MAR

# MAR

*A Glimpse into the Natural
Life of a Bird*

*Louise de Kiriline Lawrence*

**Natural Heritage/Natural History Inc.**

Toronto

published by Natural Heritage/Natural History Inc.
P.O. Box 69, Station H
Toronto, Ontario
M4C 5H7
© April 1986

First published in 1976 by Clarke, Irwin & Company Limited

Lawrence, Louise de Kiriline, 1894-
    Mar: a glimpse into the natural life of a bird
ISBN 0-920474-40-3
2. Yellow-bellied sapsucker. I. Title.
QL795.B57L39 1986   598'.72   C86-093479-9

# Contents

Books by
Louise de Kiriline Lawrence

Another Winter Another Spring
The Lovely And The Wild
The Log House Nest
Mar
The Quintuplets First Years
To Whom The Wilderness Speaks

# Foreword

I looked with eyes opened wide—and this is what I saw! I listened with ears sharply attuned—and this is what I heard!

This story is a simple narrative of a single bird's life, its naturally developed habits, desires and drives. It seeks to discover the interplay between the living creature and its environment, to determine the impact of events, trends and changes upon the individual's tolerance and responses. For therein are secreted the fundamental functions of nature and of life, of rhythm and of balance, and of their compensating effects without which no growth, no evolution is possible. Without the recognition and the knowledge of these two principles no insightful comprehension of man's relationship with his environment, with his fellow creatures and with the members of his own species can be successfully achieved.

The dramatic and the sensational seldom yield the treasures of enlightenment that the commonplace and the unpretentious often harbour unsuspected. For being as much a part of the whole as the rarity and the spectacular, the small and the ordinary miss the disadvantages of distortion and exaggeration in displaying the simple facts.

L. de K.L.

# Chapter One

## Arrival in Spring

It is mid-April. The morning dawns with the crisp chilliness typical of this northern land around Pimisi Bay in the early spring. Ice and lingering patches of snow crunch underfoot. The sun rises brilliant through the breathless mists and directs its radiance warmingly upon the land. The lake is still ice-bound, but wherever the currents are strong enough black spaces of open water form and increase. The gray-green ice, having just released its tough grip on the shores, floats on top of the rising waters.

Deep among the trees steam stands in the places where the sunshine penetrates through windows in the forest ceiling and releases the frost-bound humidity of the earth. The smells of pungent decay mingle with the spicy scents of running sap and of the sticky bracts that still enfold the virgin leaf. Life, regenerated from the dead, is clean and gainful and apt. In this gentle, timid world of early spring the sun beckons and draws and procreates with its increasingly compelling heat.

A woodpecker travels across the land with unerring instinct, a yellow-bellied sapsucker, a male recognized by its scarlet throat patch. This bird belongs to one of the two species of woodpeckers that inhabit this forest and that migrate south each fall. He flies from one tree trunk to another. Having flown all night, did he perhaps come down from out of the skies in the pre-dawn hour to rest? And as dawn breaks, he lingers, waiting for the light to increase.

The sapsucker shrugs, puffs up all his feathers and lets them fall back into place. Then he just sits, clinging to the trunk of the tree. A few specks on the bark attract his attention; he pecks at them. He looks over his shoulder. He lets go his grip and, as if pushed northwards by a force unseen, flies on.

Low through the trees the sapsucker flies, drifting along the ridge and the shore of the lake. He skirts the pine-grown hill at the south end of Pimisi Bay. Again he lingers as if to test the accuracy of his homing sense, clinging to one tree trunk, then going on to the next. He lingers again as if searching, and seems to edge his way ahead more slowly.

We meet, the sapsucker and I, where the creek swollen with spring freshets pours wildly and noisily over slimy rocks and fallen moss-covered tree trunks and stubs. A bright red band gleaming on the sapsucker's leg gives me a sudden joyous shock. I know this bird. Four springtimes ago I placed the red band on his right leg and another numbered aluminum one on the other. And then I named him Mar. Today, for the fifth time, he has come to this same forest, to the shores of this same lake. Warily I watch every move he makes to glean, if I can, the subtle nuances of his moods, the signs indicating the elemental urges and reactions that dominate and direct all his activities.

❧

One by one the landmarks of his old territory crowd in upon Mar. The sheltered bay with its wide margins of reed-grown shallows is already alive with singing red-winged blackbirds displaying their scarlet epaulets as they flit possessively over a small area of cattails. From a ditch along the road a song sparrow perched atop a tall, dead weed gives several loud songs, and a

2

nosey woodchuck looks out from behind a mound of freshly excavated saffron sand. At the edge where forest and lake meet in a tangled jumble of fallen trees and upturned roots a winter wren, tail stiffly erect over its back, holds forth in a startlingly powerful vocalization for all who wish to hear.

The stand of slender white birches on the slope attracts Mar's attention. Last summer and fall Mar and his family spent much of their time here boring row upon row of evenly spaced holes around the trunks of two or three of these trees. The sap oozed from the holes and the birds sucked it. One of the trees died during the winter from having been too heavily ringed. Mar clings to a white trunk, picks at a hole. He bores another, puts his head sideways and pries out a bit of cambium.

The territory and range Mar inhabited during the four years before stretch farther across the road over three more acres along the southeastern slope. Tall pines, balsam firs, spruces and cedars grow on this land, interspersed with aspens and birches, a second growth of almost mature forest untouched for many years and rich in stubs and debris.

The familiar sights, the well-known sounds, impinge upon Mar's awareness. The drive of his great northbound spring flight loses its impetus and dies.

❦

It is very still in the early spring morning, not a breath of wind stirs the clear, chilly air. A silent hairy woodpecker in black and white, just relieved from his night-long session on a clutch of eggs deep in his rough-hewn cavity, crosses the road in great aerial dips. Invisible from above, Mar rests, clinging to the smooth, green trunk of an aspen. The bursts of clapping noises from the hairy woodpecker's wings reach him faintly. For a second he stays motionless, tense, then relaxes again. A foursome of purple finches, two males and two females, engaged in continuous small talk among themselves, alight in the top of the aspen to pilfer tidbits from its opening catkins. Keenly alert to any unidentified movement or sound, Mar instantly flattens himself against the trunk. But the indifference of the finches soon persuades him of their harmlessness, and he settles down to preen his feathers.

Gently his bill picks among the soft plumage of his breast, under the left wing. With a lissome movement he passes his bill over the oil gland at the root of his tail. He draws one wingfeather through his bill, and restores the cohesion of all the barbs and barbules of the pinion.

Mar is in full nuptial dress. The fine erectile feathers of the frontal part of his crest glow blood red, matching the scarlet patch he wears under his chin. Below the throat patch, a jet-black band spreads in a semi-circle across his breast in striking contrast with the two areas of vivid red. Black and white geometric lines and patterns adorn his head, neck, back, wings and spiked tail. The veiling of yellowish ochre over his flanks and belly produces a subtle and beautiful counter-shading effect. And over the whole of his plumage there is a sheen as if it had been generously anointed with brilliantine.

Suddenly Mar calls, a loud *oh-weee, oh-weee, oh-weee, oh-weee.* The sound is slightly wheezy in quality, like air escaping from a pair of bellows. He repeats the four calls several times. He listens for an answer that does not come.

Mar flies a little farther into his home woods. He alights on the dry stump of a broken-off dead branch. He sets his bill and taps softly, tentatively. The dry wood resounds satisfactorily and tempts from the southern hill a soft echo. Hesitating no longer, Mar drums his full signal —a tap, a drill of tappings, followed by two or three emphasized solitary taps —a decisive, authoritative signal.

But still there is no answer. No sound betrays the presence of another sapsucker in the neighbourhood. A robin alights in the

4

top of a fir and flaps its wings anxiously as it utters a warning note. The red-winged blackbirds, the song sparrows, the winter wrens are there, but of his own species Mar is still alone.

He sinks his being into his solitude, into the illusive security of his own home grounds. He flies to the telephone pole in the very centre of his range, his favourite drumming post from last year and from all the years before that. He hops to the tip of the crossbar from which the wires hang loosely, studded with glistening dewdrops. In a familiar spot, already richly indented with last year's chisel marks of his bill, Mar raps out another triumphant announcement of his arrival home.

His first territorial mission thus fulfilled, he sidles around to the sunny side of the pole. He lifts all the feathers on his shoulders and along his back and lets the sun's rays penetrate directly upon his bare skin. He wallows in the heat, closes his eyes, opens his wings. In an ecstasy of limp enjoyment he falls to rest.

❦

The next morning I find Mar hopping along the trunk of an aspen at the forest's edge opposite the telephone pole. He props his pointed tailfeathers against the rough bark, jerks his head to give himself the necessary upward impetus, hops. His grasping feet achieve another grip a good distance farther up.

The tree is dying. Dry twigs and budless branches at the top disclose a soft and rotting core within. The trunk accommodates eight old cavities creating a system of interior apartments that for years in the past have housed various occupants from birds to flying squirrels.

These holes exercise upon Mar an extraordinary attraction. Last year he himself started one of these, but soon abandoned it. Instead he flew to the far southern end of the range and there, in a tall slender aspen, excavated his nest hole. The inside diameter of the trunk measured less than his own length of eight and half

5

inches. But, cramped space or not, from this hole in due time Mar and his mate successfully fledged their family.

And now Mar is back again at the first old tree. He spirals around the trunk. An impelling curiosity urges him on to inspect each of the eight holes. But the time has not come. Rounded apertures do not yet elicit from him a response more significant than a furtive glance inside and a few light taps on the rim of the doorway.

Suddenly a sharp loud tattoo interrupts Mar's hole inspection. The woods absorb it like a fading echo. Thoroughly aroused, Mar dashes in the direction of the signal. His wings clip at high speed in shallow beats. Halfway across the open right-of-way he veers abruptly. He swoops on to his favourite crossbar on the telephone pole and there raps out his emphatic answer. Then he waits. He listens motionless, shoulders hunched. Deep silence is his only answer.

On the road in the sun two song sparrows engage the centre of the scene. An important issue is being disputed exactly on the borderline between their territories. They face each other. They hop and they step, advancing and retreating and advancing again, executing what seems like intricate dance steps. Excitement grips one of them and he lifts his left wing high in the air. The other ballons all his body feathers; he looks like a brown ball of fluff. Thus they spar for several minutes along the common borderline. They mark it with emphasis and ostentation. Each one seeks to awe the other with his eccentric appearance. Suddenly they reach a limit of impulsion. They never come to grips. They fly apart, each one back to his own domain on opposite sides of the road. Each mounts the swaying top of a favourite bush. They break into song and the vehemence of the effort makes their tails quiver.

Mar ignores the antics of the two sparrows. He does not hear their songs. His ears are attuned to other sounds — the message that he just received. Another sapsucker drummed on his land, indicating a potential claim upon it. Or did it only mark the fact of its passage through to another goal? The silence endures.

Mar is not in the mood to pursue any further the challenge he flung upon the winds from the telephone pole. He clings to the trunk of a spiked balsam fir low among the shielding branches. Clear golden, sticky, resinous drops ooze from abrasions in the leathery bark. Mar picks out a clean spot. He cuts a square hole through the outer bark and begins eating the yellowish-white bast. He sits there for a long time. He wrenches away small bits of the highly scented stuff. And when the hole yields no more, he hops aside to start the procedure in another place.

A black-moustached male flicker has just arrived. At the poplar stub down by the lake he looks into the old nesting hole where he nested last year. But he shows no greater enthusiasm than Mar did, looking into his this morning. Lazily the flicker perches on a dead branch just above the doorway. He stretches a wing and a leg far back over his spread tail and the shafts of every stiff feather pencilled in gold flash briefly in the rays of the sun. He heard the sapsuckers exchange their signals, but they do not concern him. He moves to the top of the stub, clasps it securely with both feet. He opens his bill and utters a series of loud calls: *keck-keck-keck-keck-keck!*

Not far from the flicker, at another much slighter stub, two downy woodpeckers are highly excited. They are about to decide, once and for all, upon the exact spot to excavate their nest hole. The female makes herself fully responsible for the momentous decision. Her partner—the one with the bright red spot at the back of his head—is of scant help. He fusses about her, inordinately excited by her mere presence. He approaches her, his scarlet nape spot erect, every feather trembling. But she will have none of it. In easy long dips she flies across an ice-free scintillating bay, leaving him sitting there, all the excitement suddenly drained from him.

And then, startling by its suddenness, from the cool precincts of the brook, the winter wren bursts once again into cascades of song. The small, brown bird performs from the hidden wilderness of the forest floor with such unconcern as if the amazing syncopations and the volume of the notes were of little moment or effort.

And so for yet another day Mar's solitude remains unbroken.

❦

Softened by rain, the ice on the lake broke up under the influence of the mild spring night. The sun peered over the horizon through the humid mists that filled the air. This night of stillness, aired by hardly stirring southwesterly breezes and the rising temperature, brought about auspicious conditions for the migrating birds' northward flight. Down they came from the skies, moving across the land in wave upon wave. Some came surreptitiously, never stopping; others came slowly, lingering to feed and to rest.

Clasped tightly to the resin-oozing trunk, Mar sucks a drop of cambium-scented sap from the square hole. But it soon runs dry. He picks up a loosened piece of bast with his rough, eel-like tongue. It slips off, but is instantly scooped up by his curved wings.

A drawn-out call repeated eight times startles Mar from his feeding: *oh-weee, oh-weee, oh-weee, oh-weee!* From yet another direction comes an answering signal.

Excitement, shivering, strained alertness! Deeply stirred by these sounds, Mar flings himself into the air. Straight as an arrow he flies, shoulders hunched, wings clipping the air with exaggerated mincing movements. A superlative flourish brings him right beside one of the newly arrived sapsucker intruders that dared appear upon his private enclave.

Immediately he goes into animated display. He props his tail against the horizontal branch, he stretches his dwarflike legs to the outermost hooks of his curved claws. In a gesture full of threat and menace he lifts his bill to the heavens. In jerky, emphatic jabs his bill points right and left. All the additional movements that compose and colour his full display—the erection of his scarlet crest, his trembling, lightly fluffed red throat patch, his flicking wings, the sharp intolerant mewing noises he utters—all of these accentuate the intimidating jabbing of his bill. Markings and colourations, black, red and white, further underline the spectacular nature of these demonstrations. And all this—the movements, the attitudes, the colours—compose the full pattern of the sapsucker's most common and prominent ritual, the aggressive-social display. It is with this that he meets all comers and with this he endeavours to keep them at a distance to preserve and to assert his individual place and function in the environment.

Move for move and colour for colour the strange male sapsucker matches Mar's display. Together they advance, one ahead of the other and their voices mingle in strident, hostile noises. The third sapsucker that dared rap out his signal on Mar's territory hears the noises, sees the other two displaying. Excitement—temptation! He joins the party and the three birds outdo each other in fancy posturings. Their bills point excitedly right and left, they hop in pursuit of each other. Their agitation swells.

The anticlimax comes unexpectedly. All pause, frozen in their poses. Mar pecks hard at a small spot one inch from his grasping claws under his breast, a spontaneous movement that somewhat relieves the frustration of the moment. The intruders linger. The aggressive urge grips Mar anew. The pitch of his excitement rebuilds. He flings himself into the air in an ostentatious fluttering flight on mincing wings, giving loud cries, *weee-tick, weee-tick*. He alights with a flourish on the trunk of a neighbouring tree, his every pose and utterance an assertion of his priority on the land.

The effect upon the two intruders is instantaneous. Both alight near Mar. There a repeat performance of the entire ritual follows of such intensity and duration that it makes the ensuing pause a necessity. This provides Mar with an opportunity of success. As the three birds renew their demonstrations, Mar hops in pursuit. The intruders finally reach an ultimate point on their upward, outward arboreal paths. They take off and vanish from sight.

Mar's red crest trembles slightly and he wipes his bill thoroughly on the perch. He returns to the bast holes in the balsam fir. But he does not feed, for he has not yet regained his calm. He flies to the telephone pole, and there he raps out a resounding signal reaffirming his supremacy upon his land.

❀

During the next three days intense activities and excitement engage Mar to the uttermost of his capacities. Migrating sapsuckers continually sweep into the region and out again northwards. In response to their calls and their drummings, Mar dashes from one end of his extended range to the other. Like a winged harlequin in black and white, he flashes through the still leafless trees almost without stop or repose.

Again and again his mere presence provokes new occasions for fervid displays. Not only do they involve the repulsion and pursuit of the intruders, but they also tempt other sapsuckers, transients and neighbours, to join in the animated gatherings. Sometimes as many as half a dozen of them fill the forest with their petulant mewing noises, their flippant drumming and competitive aggressive demonstrations.

Occasionally a female intermingles with the crowd. And, except for her white throat patch, there is little either in her behaviour or fervour that separates her from the males. And thus, although possessed of the same vaguely stirring pre-nuptial urges, for a time she remains neutral and incognito among them.

Up one lane and down the other Mar patrols his land. For birds of other species he has neither eyes nor ears. His preoccupation is entirely with his own species, the only kind that is able effectively to encroach upon his living room. And often his absorption with these weighty territorial matters is so complete as to reduce to a dangerous degree his usual alertness. On one occasion, I watched with my heart in my throat his last-second dash headlong into thick cover to save himself from a pigeon hawk, the swift, little falcon that so frequently preys upon the unwary woodpecker. Another time, by madly circling around a tree trunk, he narrowly escaped the murderous talons of a large female Cooper's hawk. Had it happened when this long-tailed, short-winged foe of all smaller birds was less under the sway of her migratory urge, Mar's destiny might well have been quickly sealed.

❀

The drumming of the woodpecker functions essentially in the same way as the singing of the woodland bird. It conveys a double message. It proclaims the woodpecker's prior rights upon certain acres of land containing the facilities required for nesting and foraging. The sound sent through the forest also attracts woodpeckers of the same species. To the males it is a summons for confrontation; to the females, especially the young unattached ones, for potential pairing.

Next to the displays, the drumming is the most important part of the yellow-bellied sapsucker's territorial behaviour. It comes to the fore most prominently when, on auspicious days during migration, many other sapsuckers appear upon the scene, or when close neighbours surround the chosen range and provide frequent encounters. At such times the sapsucker's drumming becomes positively frantic. The bird races from one drumming post to the next. The post may be a loose piece of bark or a dry twig, a wooden sign or the metal part of a chimney, all situated in strategic places inside the range or somewhere near the flexible borders.

11

The female sapsucker also drums. Her drumming is principally a territorial activity that comes into effect slightly later than the male's, because after pairing takes place she often acts on behalf of the partnership while the male is otherwise engaged.

At the peak of territorial activities, sapsuckers are almost incapable of passing by any object from which they can entice a sufficiently loud and hollow sound without rapping out their challenging *ra-ta-tatatatata-ta-ta-ta*.

Four years ago, when he was an inexperienced yearling, Mar's great urge to drum conveniently delivered him bodily into my careful hands. And this is the way it happened.

In his persistent endeavour to establish himself upon the land, Mar accidentally found my spade hanging from a nail in a tree. It had a wooden handle. For half a minute or so he clung to the trunk of the tree hesitating, looking at the handle. Then he leaned over and rapped out a smart signal on the spade handle. It gave off a resounding tattoo that carried far into the forest. Mar listened attentively, his crest on end, as the echo of his own drumming faded in the distance. His eyes shone, he postured with his back depressed. Even as the drummings of his fellows excited him, so the sound of his own drumming obviously affected him, perhaps as a natural result of the cumulative effects of the springtime's deepening agitations.

I thought of the possibility of catching the sapsucker in the woodpecker trap, an oblong wire box installed on the trunk of a tree not far away. A woodpecker, entering it from below, would trip the door shut. Very gradually, I moved the spade toward the trap.

Perceiving the disappearance of his new drumming post, Mar did not take long to discover where it had gone. Indeed, the vanishing act doubled his urge to drum. He dashed in pursuit of the spade. He rapped out one loud triumphant tattoo after the other upon it.

Again I moved the spade. This time Mar found it sooner than

the first time. Obviously, the mobility of the spade did not in the least affect his overpowering impulse to make himself heard. Nor did the banding trap attached above it bother him. With his usual flourish he alighted upon the handle and played a vigorous tattoo. And then, in accordance with long established habit, he hopped upwards. With a faint click the trap closed upon him.

The next instant, suddenly shorn of all his dash and dominance, the beautiful bird lies in my hand. One intense urge to live and to escape pervades him. But he makes not a move. Not a feather quivers to betray his paralyzing fear. With his feet drawn tightly into his soft belly feathers, he lies there petrified. His brown eyes are soft as velvet, lustrous with animation, as I mark him for life with a red band.

I open my hand to release him. For an instant, he feels himself captive and lies motionless in my open palm. Slowly I roll him over right side up. In a flash he is gone.

A second later I hear his loud emphatic rataplan on a signboard close by. But with the horrifying experience of hopping into a trap, Mar's infatuation with the spade handle as a drumming post is destroyed forever.

# Chapter Two

## The Female's Journey

**W**hen the days are slowly beginning to lengthen in the deep south of North America, the female yellow-bellied sapsucker falls prey to a curious restlessness. She flits from tree to tree. She feeds a little, preens a little. But the disquiet that seems to pervade her whole system especially at night will not leave her. It is as if an as yet faint desire to take wing, to move away, possessed her. But the impulse is not sufficiently strong to turn the mood into action.

Then suddenly, one day, she finds herself surrounded by flocks of strange birds. They swarm around her restlessly, nervously. They are hungry and settle down to feed eagerly. Some are tired and quickly go to sleep, head tucked away, oblivious, lost in an ethereal nap that quickly restores drained energies.

The lively movements and sociabilities of these mercurial woodland birds around her, their soft cheeping and singing, have an intensifying effect on the sapsucker's own state of agitation. A strangely urgent impulse seizes her to move on with them. But before her motivation comes alive, they are gone as suddenly as they came, leaving her bewildered and alone. And the familiarity with the place where she lived and fed and roosted through the

15

months while the sun was low once again tightens its hold on her and holds her captive.

But the gatherings of birds continue to move into her area and out again. And gradually her mood changes and her resistance against their enticement weakens. Her day comes finally, when at last she flits away, drawn northwards. And as she moves, she is nervous, excited, and her crest, blood-red, is on end. She is free. And gradually the migratory impulse within her grows stronger, more buoyant, irresistible.

The unknown imbues her with an acute sense of insecurity. She becomes intensely responsive to her changing environment, alert to all the dangers that may lurk there. She flies on from one landmark to the next, always northwards. She is in the company of other birds. Sometimes they surround her in great numbers. At other times their numbers thin out until she is aware of only one or two companions. She sees them moving, she hears their calls. But now her drive is so strong and unremitting, that even were she all alone she still would fly on into the deep of the night, guided unerringly by an internal compass toward the set goal in the far north. And with the sun at her back she would travel as if along a clearly blazed path, the path chosen by her forebears since time immemorial and coded upon her nervous system as an indelible imprint.

So, with the great flocks of migrating birds, the female sap-sucker travels northwards in the wake of the greening season. She feels her way, flying by day closer to the ground and, taking her time, she stops, feeds and rests with the others. Sometimes at night she takes to the air and it is full of birds. Aided by auspicious winds, they fly under the vault of darkness from the south to the north.

Then a change suddenly interrupts the migrants. Set in motion by the circulating winds behind a played-out storm, a flow of icy northerly air throws up a barrier of cold weather into their path and forces them to a halt. Only a few intrepid spirits, hardier

16

and more adaptable than the others, pass the barrier and fly on bravely but without assurance of survival as the reward for their imprudent hurry. Others, suddenly drained of their northward drive, about-turn and fly back with the sun in their faces until warming trends once again reverse their impulse.

Behind the barrier of cold air the concentration of birds pouring through the good weather zones in the south swells into a baffled, tension-ridden throng. They spread out over a broad front while the break in the weather is delayed. When it comes at last, late but inevitable, overwhelming the flow of cold air, an avalanche of birds is released; they sweep across the land, northwards, along the surface of the earth, in the air, never stopping.

Caught in this stream of northbound birds, the female sapsucker flies on cross-country. She keeps to the tree-covered areas where most of her emergency larders are stored, through orchards and woods. She follows the ridges, the slopes, the rivers and the shores of the lakes. She shares with the others their excitements, their dangers and their irresistible urge to press on northwards.

On a soft mild morning in early May the female sapsucker approaches a small glassy bay more than a thousand miles from where she first set out on her prodigious journey. This bay is part of the lovely northern lake of Pimisi Bay that lies girdled by the undulating shorelines of little bays and inlets, and framed by tall, dark green forests.

Is it a vague feeling of familiarity dawning upon her that makes her slacken her speed northwards? Is it a memory, half nebulous, yet compelling, of the features of this land, its contours and it fragrances, of its waters and trees and slopes, that causes her to linger? Is it the image of this land indelibly imprinted upon her memory that enables her once again to find this tiny spot on the vast map of this northern wilderness where, exactly a year ago, she came and settled for the first time, where she mated and raised her young?

How does it work, this all but miraculous sense of orientation

17

in the migrating bird? What, in essence, is this extraordinary homing sense, that with overwhelming precision guides the migrating bird at the right time alternatively northwards or southwards? How did this sure directional sense imbedded into endless generations of migrating birds evolve? So many have endeavoured to understand this riddle of nature, but, like a will-o'-the-wisp, the key to it still eludes explanation. No doubt it is based on one of those logical mechanisms of nature, intrinsically simple and self-evident, as are all her intricate workings and interactions once their secrets are revealed.

❧

Rain had fallen during the night when I first encountered the female sapsucker as she came along in the morning. Warm, drenching showers had saturated the receptive earth and accumulated in heavy drops that still clung to the branches and twigs.

The buds of the trees were swelling. The quaking aspens, always in a hurry to put on their spring finery, were beginning to swathe themselves in the sheerest green. Sweet white violets and blue hepaticas peered from under the dead leaves and in a patch of green wet moss goldthreads eagerly opened their white faces to the sun, shining like stars.

Aimlessly, listlessly, the sapsucker meandered from tree to tree, clinging to the upright trunks. The power and the great propulsion of her migratory drive was gradually evaporating. She preened a feather on her breast, picked a little under one wing. Nimbly she brought her right foot under her wing and scratched the side of her head. For a while that was all she wanted to do.

The rhythmic drumming of a sapsucker somewhere to her right, ending with three slow taps, aroused her. This was followed by eight wheezy calls. The female sat up, she listened intently, her head slightly cocked. Eagerly she searched for a good spot to drum upon, found it and drummed. Having thus fulfilled her part of the communication, she sat perfectly still, as if waiting for what was to follow.

Suddenly she drops to the underside of the branch on which she is sitting. There she hides, motionless, feathers tightly pressed against her slim body.

Two sapsuckers swoop on to the branch. One has a red throat patch, the other a white one. Oblivious to all things except themselves, the pair engages in a series of frivolous displays above the hiding female. Their wings are slightly opened with the tips crossed over the rump. Their tails are trailing stiffy against the horizontal branch. The birds point their heads and bills heavenward with great enthusiasm in rhythmically jerky bobbing motions right and left. All of this is accompanied by soft mewing notes. The pointing gestures suggest hostility but the soft mewing notes are unmistakably friendly, and together they lend a gloriously ambiguous extravagance to the whole show. Each movement, each detail, and the way and the varying intensity with which they are performed correspond closely with the birds' reactions to each other, with the changing circumstances and events.

The play of the pair highly excites the female sapsucker hiding under the branch. She responds to the convivial movements and posturings of the two black and white and red birds dancing above her and to the sound of their notes; she can contain herself no longer. She dashes out from hiding and joins in the displays, bobbing, jerking her head left and right, fanning her tail. Every movement she makes matches the movements of the pair, and the degree of her animation is equal to their fervour. She is driven by an urgency as definite and as compelling as the one that just brought her to these northern parts from the far south.

At the sight of her, the pair increases the tempo and the vehemence of the displays. Together the three birds perform their characteristic rites, this meeting between a resident pair and a stranger, with utter abandon.

19

Finally the male, with his red crest on end and his red throat patch fluffed, calls the end to the performance. Off he flies, his wings ostentatiously fluttering, his head low. And behind him trails the insistent, enticing sound of his loud seesawing come-on call: *weee-hick, weee-hick, weee-hick!* His female darts off in pursuit.

Before the other female sapsucker has time to catch up with the pair at their new display arena, her excitement wanes abruptly. Once again she gives in to the mood of moving on, and she flies slowly, searchingly from tree to tree. She stops or preens, she feeds, she just sits there, for the last bit of energy that sustained her long flight throughout the past weeks is being slowly drained from her.

She reaches the tall, half-dead aspen with the eight holes bored into its decaying core. She observes them attentively. Obviously they impress her as being worthy of investigation. She clings to the opening of one of them and looks in. Then she passes on to another.

Her predilection for old holes, so prominent a trait in all adult sapsuckers, makes her linger for a while. But no! This is not the right place. And she flies on again, crossing the road.

❦

The rough ground strewn with boulders, the woodland debris collected in thick soft mounds on the forest floor, attract her. This is to her familiar surroundings. There is the ravine thickly grown with soft maples, honeysuckle and hazel bushes. There is the enormous white spruce whose dense drooping branches shine almost blue in the sun and provide security and shelter for so many so often. At its feet lies the prostrate trunk of a dead aspen, felled by the wind and its own rot. The curly paper bark of a slender white birch wafts lightly in the wind and a bit higher up, just before the branching begins, five strands of rounded holes, her very own borings in search of sap, encircle the trunk like

20

pearls on a string. By some subtle sense which we have difficulty to define objectively, the female sapsucker recognizes all this.

The sight of the jumbled landscape brings out within her a memory so vivid that it makes her stop. Now she is no longer hesitant, she moves no longer searchingly, aimlessly. She flies directly to a tall and very slender aspen standing at the crest of the slope down to the ravine. One single hole in its bole, facing east, pierces the gray-green trunk.

She clings to the edge of the worn doorway. She looks in, she makes one move as if intending to go in, one hesitating move, before she pops within. And if, watching her, I did not already know that this very cavity was the one she nested in last year, the decisiveness with which she acted would have given me ample evidence that she was indeed at home. This land with the stubs and the bushes and the rocks and the trees, cut into a small ravine, is hers, the spot remembered. It belongs to her and she inseparably belongs to it for life.

Another aspen attracts her attention. There a piece of dry wood, very thin, buckles partly detached from the trunk. She flies there, clings to it. She gathers her feet under her and with the assured gesture of one having tapped in the precise place uncounted times in the past, she sets her bill and raps out her full accented drumming signal.

For a while nothing but silence reigns. A red squirrel races up the trunk of the female's old nesting tree. It chatters to itself and casts a hurried glance inside the hole. The sapsucker interrupts herself in the middle of a drumming signal. She is on the point of flying at the red intruder, but she withholds her attack. The squirrel runs down the trunk, indifferent to everything but its own moods and movements.

The female sapsucker, pacified, continues to sit. She tucks one foot into her belly feathers. She half closes her eyes, she dreams, rests and awakens. She grasps the trunk with both feet, sets her bill and drums tattoo after tattoo at measured intervals. When

21

she has finished, she just sits.

Just sitting! How often have I observed this sudden stop of all activity in the midst of intense action! A period of total, self-preserving rest, a refuelling of the physical energies, never more competently practised than by the animals in the wild! Suddenly, the peace is broken. Mar must have heard the sound of the female's drumming. It excites him. Although in the midst of an encounter with a transient intruder, he leaves the stranger to its own devices. He bursts in upon the scene at the ravine. With a resounding flop he alights on the trunk not far from the female. Scarlet crest stiffly erect, throat patch like an unruly red beard sprouting in all directions, he drums. Instantly the female moves toward him. But before she reaches him he is gone, squealing, with the female in hot pursuit.

In a tall pine whose spreading volume encompasses the whole immediate environment, the two birds meet on an horizontal branch. They are in animated display. A bright beam of the sun spotlights the pair as they posture and move, bobbing in jerky rhythm, advancing together and retreating. Light shivers run through their stiffened feathers and suggest the intensity of the nervous tension that possesses them. The intrusion they mutually inflict upon each other's domains inevitably puts them in an aggressive mood. I can see it in the way they posture and move, I can hear it in the sharp tone of their voices.

Thus, once again, these two meet in the same place where they lived together in another year, after an absence and a separation of seven months. No memory breaks through the impact of the immediate situation and they respond to it spontaneously. Their former intimate relationship as fully cooperating mates developed from their rituals and their courtship, their nest preparations, the shared incubation of their eggs and the arduous labours caring for and fledging their young ones. Now all this is as if it had never been. Only I know that Mar, with his red leg band and the female with her green one met before and then became an inseparable team engaged in the fulfilling of the reproductive functions laid down within them.

To Mar today the female is nothing but an intruder upon his land. She is a sapsucker like all the others, clad in black and white and red, and behaving like one. She is one of his own species, whose presence he would naturally protest. And the white throat patch she carries as distinguishing mark of her sex means nothing at that moment. To the female Mar appears as a double, whose proximity excites her and who tempts her to join in the ambiguous antics of these aggressive-social displays. The displays are meant to repel. And in the present situation, the time, the moods of the birds, correspond with this message.

Mar advances toward the female, and together they stage a vigorous display, bobbing, bills pointing right and left, tails spread and backs deeply depressed. It takes them tandem-wise along the branch to the accompaniment of shrill mewing notes. Irresistibly attracted by these movements and noises two other sapsuckers join in the demonstrations. The four birds perform together, each one contributing by pose and by movement to the intensifying vehemence and excitement of all the others. In the spring the time allotted the migrating sapsucker to achieve secure territorial standing and to conclude successfully its courtship is very short. It is an intense and a hurried process.

Mar breaks up the party. He darts to his favourite telephone pole, uttering his longdrawn squealing flightsong. He raps out his drumming signal, his emphatic declaration of possession of these forested acres.

The next instant the female is beside him. Mar advances upon her, he attempts to chase her away. But the female stands her ground. She shows no timidity, she neither advances nor retreats. Somehow this attitude drains part of the aggressiveness from both of them. For a moment their mutual responses are in perfect balance.

This time the female makes the break. With hunched shoulders, she flits off on mincing wings, emitting the squealing flightsong. She puts on a highly extravagant show; every movement is exaggerated, every utterance is strongly accented. This formal ritual is full of meaning, and it belongs to her and to the species and to the moment. She shoots across the road, straight as an arrow, back to the old nest tree by the ravine.

Half a second later Mar is beside her. Again they display in unison. This time they posture opposite each other, bobbing, facing each other, heads swishing right and left, wings partially opened, flapping gently. Mar dashes away.

The female clings to the doorway and looks into the rotting hole. She flies to her drumming post and drums. Mar's answering tattoo comes to her from across the road, slightly muffled by the distance.

Thus ended Mar's and the female's first meeting on the same territorial range where last year they came together and nested and raised their family.

Their good luck in surviving the dangers of their migration across the continent, their uncanny ability to find their way, and the fidelity that attaches the yellow-bellied sapsucker to the land it occupied during its first breeding season, all contribute to the auspicious meeting.

On these premises the coming together again of the members of a pair each year in the same place for so long as they live is inevitable. The personal attachment between the two is only a secondary matter that needs reaffirmation in due course.

# Chapter Three

## The Creation of a Home

The female sapsucker lost no time establishing her own personal territory upon Mar's range. By this move she clearly indicated her intention to stay. Her choice was self-evident. Here was the tree in which Mar last year excavated their nest cavity. Within it she dropped her first clutch of eggs. Here she established her favourite drumming post, on which now once again she liked to sound her signals. This land was hers. She delineated it with her movements; she confirmed her ownership by her drumming and her presence. And she put her seal upon the land by refusing to be intimidated and chased from it.

❧

With these moves Mar's female followed the general habit of female sapsuckers which as first-year newcomers or as returning old-timers enter upon a male's range. For a while they remain within this limited area, making their sorties to join in the aggressive-social displays, in the initiating courtship rituals. Then, as the pairbond between the two strengthens, the female's tendencies to segregation gradually evaporate. The living room a pair of sapsuckers requires during the breeding season extends over five to seven acres. In the strict sense this is not a consistently defended area. The sapsuckers' claim upon it is only valid with respect to other sapsuckers; other birds, including woodpeckers, usually enjoy unchallenged access. The sapsucker asserts his occupancy by drumming. Like a walkie-talkie, it acts by remote control calling trespassers of his own species to show. The trespassers are then drawn into series of highly ritualistic displays which serve primarily to dissipate nervous tensions. Seldom, except under special circumstances, does the situation reach the point of outright battle.

Unlike the range, the territory is a consistently defended area. It is a constricted area radiating some fifty to one hundred feet from the selected nest tree.

As the sapsuckers' interest begins to centre around nest preparations, the territory acquires increased significance. There the sapsuckers reign supreme. They become stealthy and surreptitious. On the least provocation they aggressively defend the territory against all woodpeckers and hole-nesters. When nervous tensions run high, the birds become fiercely intolerant of any intentional or innocent approach to the nest tree; any creature that comes too close lays itself open to immediate and savage attack.

The stratagem of the sapsuckers' defence varies. The male usually stalks the enemy, peering forth from behind the tree trunks. When danger threatens nest and contents, he darts inside, turns around and sits waiting behind the doorway for the advent of the enemy, sharp bill poised at the ready.

The female usually deals with trespassers directly by outright attack. And on occasion, when she and the male join forces, even the oversized enemy may have difficulty resisting the dashing bill-stabbing attacks of the two angry and mutually inciting defenders.

❁

From her temporary territory Mar's female sallies forth to challenge any bird of her own species and sex that enters the range. These meetings always turn into lively and highly impassioned social-aggressive parties. Noisy and provocative, they attract all other sapsuckers within earshot, neighbours as well as trespassers.

In the natural course of these events their mutual opposition to others of their kind throws Mar and his female repeatedly together, red crests on end, bobbing, jabbing their bills right and left, tails trailing. The usefulness of these repeated encounters is two-fold: they prevent hostilities from exploding into open, devastating warfare and at the same time bridge the gulf of personal antagonism between the pair, bringing them closer as co-operating partners. And thus the link of the pairbond is forged.

In the opening scenes of the sapsuckers' courtship the female acts with playful timidity. Territorial incitements and awakening sexual impulses drive her. She hides under the branches while the male protagonists in display surge back and forth above. All her feathers flattened, she looks slim and smooth. Now she is aggressive, now withdrawing, and the ambiguity pulls her from one extreme to the other. She bursts forth, joining the males in brief abandoned display, the next moment to beat a hasty retreat behind her branch.

The result of these exercises is nervous tension mounting to such a high pitch that relief becomes imperative. The end arrives abruptly. Squealing loudly, one or all the birds leave the scene of action and fly to another tree, there to stage another social-aggressive pantomime.

What role Mar's red throat patch and the female's white one played in the process of the birds recognizing each other as members of opposite sex is not clear. The sight of the male's inflated red throat may have excited the female and her white chin may have aroused him. But likely it was neither so simple nor so abrupt as this. Rather Mar's distinctly male behaviour, his patrolling the range, his drumming and calling, and the role he played in the demonstrations eventually caused the female to recognize in him a mate. And the female's behaviour within her personal area to which she always returned, her refusal to be chased away, the dissimilarities in her attitudes when they met, may well have persuaded Mar of the inevitable. And, as they continued to meet more frequently, their full recognition of each other, based on colour, pattern, form and voice, became as unavoidable as their separate returns had been to the same breeding range.

The time came when the female began to emerge from her special territory on increasingly less provocation. Her involvement in the excitements of the premises increased. The demonstrations in which they both took so ardent a part warmed them to each other's presence. The self-preserving antagonism that each bird had instinctively resorted to in defence of itself against the other slowly wore away. And thereafter, quite naturally, by maintaining their common living room inviolate against others of their own kind, they found a common interest that drew them still closer together.

Once they reached this stage, their behaviour changed in other ways as well. Although it never disappeared entirely, their aggressiveness toward each other diminished markedly. Now, whenever they met, they exchanged soft mewing notes, each acknowledging thereby the right of the other to be there, recognizing each other as mates. Their displays took on other meanings, in which the friendly social aspect became more marked. Now they faced each other in strutting competition, breasts puffed out, heads bobbing in unison, and the rivalry expressed in their movements became wheedling, seductive. When the excitement of their displays reached climax and escape became a necessity, the mincing flight and the wheezy flightsong were less challenging, but more a declaration of ingratiating incitement.

And with each performance, these highly ritualized courting displays increased in intensity and persuasiveness.

✿

Blessed springtime! The sun pours its heady radiation on everything that grows and lives. The water laps gently against the shoreline and offers its dewy humidity to the limpid air. Wakerobins nod red heads in full-blown opulence, the grass is green and the newborn bracken stems shoot through the deep cover of dead brown leaves, curled like snail's houses. The red loam, thrown up by the burrowing woodchuck, sends out a moist, pungent odour that mingles with the faint, exquisite fragrances of spring violets and the new green leaves.

Mar is possessed by a desire to investigate holes. Gaping at him, their dark interiors have a special appeal to him. He thrusts his head inside, withdraws it again. He goes in, but only to hop out again.

Memories from other years spent upon these premises pursue him. He finds the loose piece of bark in the black ash that he used to tap on, and there he drums. He darts to the bird-house by the shed, and he sounds a resonant *ra-ta-ta-ta* on its wooden wall. Down by the lake he sweeps up on the no trespassing sign, and there he drums. And on his way around he adds in passing a few more drumming posts to his extended system of communication.

On these spirited dashes from one end of the range to the other Mar comes across many trees with holes in their trunks. Other woodpeckers drilled some of these, nuthatches and chickadees excavated others, and some he bored himself. He inspects them all. But the great urgency to create for himself and a family a home still remains too diffused by other issues — patrolling the land, drumming, chasing intruders, displaying. And for a while these activities absorb his time and energies with little left for the investigation of nest holes.

The arrival of the female brings about a great change. The sight fills the male with excitement. A potent dose of renewed energy refuels his latent interest in nest holes. Her presence stirs him to search for a good nesting place, and this develops into an impulse so self-evident, so powerful that it leaves him little incentive for his former entirely absorbing territorial activities.

Down by the lakeshore a tall slender aspen in a grove of ashes, willows and cedars takes his fancy. The smooth trunk is olive green and Mar strikes upon it his first chisel mark.

A tiny drop of clear sap oozes reluctantly from the elongated, hardly visible wound. Mar taps, and with a smart twist of his bill he pries loose a chip of white wood covered with a piece of redolent, juicy bark. The act excites him. With his crest on end he hitches a foot or so down the trunk, lifting his tail quickly at each drop to prevent it from getting in the way. He leans sideways and taps in a new place, making several indentations. He hitches around to still another place on the north side and taps there. But the first place pleases him best. He hops back to it and for a minute drills energetically, leaving a perceptible depression right in the middle of a circle of chisel markings. He stops and gives four loud calls: *oh-weee — oh-weee — oh-weee — oh-weee!* The utterance is insistent, the tone slightly nasal.

From the direction of the female's territory a drumming signal reaches him, somewhat delayed, faint because of the distance. Mar clings to the tree trunk motionless.

A minute rolls by. Nothing happens. Suddenly, there is the sound of wings. This excites him. The female sweeps into sight. But, before she has time to alight beside him, Mar has gone into a behaviour sequence of high symbolic content. His bill, set at a precise angle under his breast, taps fast and persuasively on the lower edge of the just started, and as yet hardly visible, hole. Is it an invitation to her? The doorway — here — look! His red crest trembles. She edges close to him, very close, clings motionless beside him, head and bill pointing skywards, all her feathers

30

tightly compressed along her slim body. Her pose is submissive, his, with wings slightly opened and dropped and the tips elegantly crossed over his shiny rump, full of sexual meaning. The tension between them builds up, his tapping reaches a rapturous climax in force and speed. He dashes away, wings beating in a mincing moth flight, and the notes of his loud *wheee*-ing flightsong trail behind him, suspended in the air.

He darts back to the slender aspen by the lake, and all his movements are full of emphasis and ardor. But the female is not there, and his mood, still touched with residual excitation, tempts him to call once again. He waits, but there is no answer.

The attraction of her own tree, her own territory has the female captive. She flies to the nest hole. She hops to a spot just above it and pecks there. Is she going to start her own hole? But, no, the impulse is halting and desultory. Yet she remains, for she cannot tear herself away from this environment so strongly imprinted upon her memory.

A female sapsucker flies by — and this excites her, distracts her. She darts in pursuit, quivering with a suddenly aroused zeal. Now she has an active partnership in this range beyond her own premise. With unrestrained audacity she engages the trespasser, and the more excited she becomes, the more exaggerated are her movements. She dances along the branch emitting loud protesting noises, bobbing, jerking her head and bill right and left. Now she, too, exercises her priority over the land and defends it, as Mar did before she arrived.

Meanwhile Mar drills ever deeper into the green wood of the tall slender aspen by the lakeshore. For several days he works there alone. Gradually he is able to disappear inside to the tip of his tail. Drilling in green wood is laborious and his progress is slow. Often, when the female fails to appear, his interest lags. He becomes tired and listless and goes off to feed and rest.

He calls again loudly. But there is no answer. He darts away, he searches her out and displays to her. He flies off toward the

31

slender aspen, singing: *wheee-tik —wheee-tik —wheee-tik!* But she does not come. Only in a rare moment of weakening resistance she allows him to persuade her with his antics to visit him and the tree. On these occasions she clings beside him briefly while he, trembling with agitation, performs the ritual tapping ceremony at the edge of the new doorway. But the next instant she is gone again, frivolous and capricious as her moods are at this time.

For seven long days the pair indulge in this kind of behaviour while the female persists in her obstinate refusal to accept Mar's chosen nest site. But on the seventh day, suddenly there is a change. Goaded by some unknown impulse, Mar takes it into his head to visit another aspen.

This tree stands high on the southeastern slope, if not actually in the female's territory, then not far from it. The tree is dying. A colony of small black ants have happily installed themselves in its soft rotting core. A gaping hole facing south, drilled a few years ago by another pair of sapsuckers, beckons him. He looks in, but withdraws again and spends some time visiting the female, displaying. A short while later, as if inspired by some new urgency, he begins to drill a new hole through the soft wood two and a half feet above the old cavity. Down near the ground, the small black ants pour from their own private exit, some of them burdened with tiny white pupae, to seek a safer and more tranquil abode.

❦

In the spring seven days is a long time during which many things can happen. The sun shines warmer. The light green leaves begin to rustle with soft musical sounds, stirred by the warm breezes that run through the tops of the trees and are gone.

These are magic days of great movement sprung from the puzzling twist in the general scheme of nature that brings winged creatures from one end of the land to the other for no reason except to reproduce. And they come, the whip-poor-wills, the swifts, hummingbirds, flycatchers, thrushes, vireos and warblers to fill the northern forests during their brief and hectic breeding season with their ethereal presence and their rich and varied dawn choruses.

Why do they come so far? Why do they come at all? Is it to find cooler, roomier surroundings, the fresh, untouched resources of foods that the northern summer produces in such profusion at the very time when their young fill to capacity every cavity and nest hole, every scrape on the ground? Or is it to generate the kind of living species that are more vigorous and able through struggle and passionate exertion to beget a breed more viable than they are themselves?

The female sapsucker does not escape the changes arising from the advances of spring. Familiarity spurs audacity. Limits expand. Where restraint earlier kept her attached to a certain restricted area, she soon emerges master of the range. Now she, too, patrols the land with all the impetuosity of acknowledged ownership. It takes her like a rocket from one place to the other, from one drumming post to the next. Now she challenges intruders of her own species and sex and engages them in animated displays. And so, while Mar is busy expending great amounts of energy working on the cavity, the female takes over the duties he is forced to leave undone.

This is the first move made toward the establishment of the necessary sensitive interplay of reactions between the two members of the pair. Soon it develops into a teamwork of high quality and reliability, without which success in the great enterprise of reproduction could hardly be attainable. It is designed to work on the compensatory principle, so that whenever circumstances tie one of the partners to some urgent extra-curricular activity, the other one automatically takes over to fulfil routine duties. In this way subtle responses are gradually developed in both partners, allowing them to cope successfully with the pressures of time and environment and the various hazards attached to the raising of their family.

Under the new schedule the female soon finds Mar's second selected nest site. She hears him calling, she hears the sound of his drilling, of his soft *tap-tap-tap-tap-tap*. No longer confined in spirit or movement to one single area, she arrives at the nest. Mar has flown, but the gaping doorway attracts her. She clings to it, she looks in, once, several times. And then as if perfectly satisfied with what she saw, she hops under a nearby knob. It screens her from prying eyes above, and here she sits and picks daintily among the feathers on her breast.

A sight, a sound, suddenly distracts her and she dashes off. But she returns again and again. Often while Mar goes away to feed and to rest, she stays at the nest hole. Let no one come too close uninvited!

One day the excavation reaches the point when the hole is large enough for Mar to turn around inside. That night, for the first time, he sleeps in the cavity. In the morning the female arrives from her roosting place, calling loudly all the way. Here she comes! Aroused and excited, Mar goes into the ritual tapping routine inside the cavity at the edge of the opening. The female clings to the doorway and she hears the spaced tapping and sees Mar's shadowy head inside moving in the prescribed rhythm. She is pushed aside as Mar darts out and away. But this time, with no hesitation, no abortive movements popping her head in and out, she goes in. For the first time the female actually settles down to work on the cavity, tapping and drilling and throwing out chips that float to earth on small erratic drafts.

From then on the hole is as much the female's property as Mar's. But even after they reach this stage in their relationship, he spends three times as much time as the female does, working on the nest. In the sapsucker family, as in the families of the hairy and downy woodpeckers and the flickers, the male is the great nest-builder.

There are many different ways of creating and possessing, and the female's way is not the same as the male's. The dissimilarity is an asset that, rather than separating them, moulds the partners into a team. The result is an increased mutual tolerance and a closer and more efficient co-operation between them, destined eventually to achieve the fine synchronization of their sexual drives, the intimate climax of their relationship.

❧

The migration of the birds is approaching its end, and nobody knows where he came from, uninvited and unwelcome. Mar is about to add the last drilling touches to the nearly completed nest cavity. In several respects the fact that the sapsucker breeding season is thus far advanced plays an important role in the final outcome of this unexpected intrusion.

The strange male sapsucker introduces himself upon Mar's private premises without ceremony. He is in a hurry. By lucky chance I catch sight of the leg bands he is wearing, which identify him as a young bird hatched and raised on the neighbouring range last summer. He is not the first year-old sapsucker I have known to return from its initial migration to the same area where it emerged from the nest.

Obviously, this young bird has yet to find and to carve out for himself a suitable living room. Naturally, therefore, he must now be possessed by exceptionally strong and urgent territorial and sexual impulses. And this, certainly, accounts for the persistence of his behaviour.

The young bird has the brash audacity to alight beside the female as she clings to the nest entrance. And the female, with all the prerequisites present, the doorway and the partner, promptly goes into the tapping ritual—what else can she do? The next instant she is gone and the loud inciting notes of her flightsong resound in her wake. The young male pursues her—what else can he do? The two meet on a horizontal branch in full view of Mar and engage in a series of animated displays.

Like a bolt from heaven, Mar strikes. His violent attack unseats the stranger, and the two meet on another branch in a rousing highly aggressive display. They thrust their bills vigorously right and left, they bob, their wings flick, stiff tails trailing behind them. The vehemence of the two birds is at the boiling point. And all their rivalry, all their pugnacity, are gloriously embodied in their magnificent strutting movements. At that very moment under the spell of the powerful provocation, an equipoise of movement and motivation is created and maintained so finely drawn as to prevent the two birds from being precipitiously thrown into bloody bodily combat. Then, without affecting the margins of balance, the female joins in the displays of the two males.

Lacking the incentive of territorial ownership to sustain him, the young bird breaks off the displays. He darts away with Mar, screaming his challenging flightsong, in hot pursuit. The chase is on. The performance that ensues is the ultimate in avian dash and skillful aerial maneuvring. At incredible speed the two birds sweep in tight circles through the tree tops, then down through the understory. Mar, three wingbeats behind the intruder, maintains this distance constant between them as if by ordinance. They shoot past me and I hear the wind whining through their flight feathers. Without impeding their headlong fling, their wings clip a leaf here, a twig there, with the report of a toy gun. The pursuit goes on until finally both birds slam their bodies on to a branch almost simultaneously. They go into a display as intensely demonstrative as their emotional pitch is at that crucial instant.

The female, the focal point of the males' rivalry, clings beside the doorway of the nest and lets the mad race revolve about and past her in round upon round. Again she joins briefly in the displays. Again the chase is on and she is left beside the nest to

36

mark the target. Unexpectedly the young bird dashes from sight and Mar seizes the opportunity to race around his array of drumming posts and on each one rap out a clamorous fanfare. The meaning is unmistakable: Mar resides here — this room is his — let no one dare encroach upon these premises marked by his vibrant presence!

For three days the fight between Mar and the intruder goes on with unabated fury from early morning until sunset. The finishing work on the cavity is interrupted, the pair's well established routines of feeding, resting and courting are upset. On the fourth day a slight change occurs. The young bird leaves the scene of battle for prolonged periods. This lulls the vigilance of the pair and, rather hesitantly at first, they momentarily fall back into their prescribed activities.

But the peace is not to be trusted. Back comes the young bird, daringly courting the female in exciting displays. Caught unawares inside the cavity, Mar takes a second or two to react to the sounds that reach him from the outside. He explodes from the doorway, screaming his challenge. And the spectacular chase is on again.

For a long week the young bird continues to hover in the wings of the sapsuckers' stage, sometimes gone out of sight, then coming back again. In the midst of the most sensitive period of their breeding cycle, this alien and unwanted presence persists in causing highly disorganizing disruptions in the normal life and preoccupations of the pair. But the young one is working against time and overwhelming odds. At this advanced stage of the season no interloper, save death itself, can force a break between a team of paired sapsuckers and their established living space. Gradually Mar's opposition wears down the young bird's incentive to interfere and he vanishes not to return.

# Chapter Four

# The Quiescent Interval

The creative power of early summer is in evidence everywhere, strong, irresistible, indestructible. The forest is full of life and of the hush-hush promotion of new life in various stages.

In the tall aspen farther down the slope from Mar's and the female's nest tree young things are already filling the bottom of the hairy woodpeckers' nest hole behind their doorway hidden under a protruding knob. Eggs are in the downy woodpeckers' cavity excavated at a lofty height in the knotty dead stub, already riddled with holes dug by previous tenants in years past. At the top of a three-foot birch stub in an unsightly hole with ragged edges, a mother black-capped chickadee is warmly covering an over-generous clutch of ten white eggs marked with fine dots in reddish-brown. And in the red-breasted nuthatch's trim abode, drilled into the barkless trunk of a slender poplar that died young, eggs are just about to hatch behind a doorway liberally smeared with sticky scented pitch of the balsam fir.

Not more than twenty feet from Mar's and the female's tree a crooked half-hollow, entirely innocent-looking old stub leans over near collapse from advanced rot. Behind the dark gaping hole on its east side, in a red squirrel's well padded apartment, the first litter of the season, born in April, is acquiring the finishing trim and polish from their irascible, but solicitous, mother. And it is high time for them. In less than two weeks the mischievous foursome will be ready to emerge from their hot and somewhat disorderly natal environment to cavort on their own in the free, open world.

Everywhere there is haste and industry. Thinning groups of migrants on a schedule for later arrival than the rest are now dispersing through the northern forest. Immediately they start hurried initial preparations for their short nesting season. A male red-eyed vireo is reciting brief lilting songs in endless repetition as in a leisurely fashion he meanders through the tops of the highest trees to advertise his claim to this particular piece of land. A female veery, in light cinnamon-brown plumage, hops about with softly bouncing movements the way thrushes do. She carries a large, dead leaf to a slightly elevated platform at the foot of five birch stems sprouting from the same root, which she has just designated as her nest site. Her immediate neighbour, the oven-bird, steps daintily amid the forest debris, picking a straw here, a dead leaf there. She collects all of them in her bill, before transporting them under a tentlike recess formed by stiff stalks of bracken still covered with the frazzled dead leaves of last summer, there to start her oven-shaped nest.

All over, the forest territories are held and defended by their owners against intruders belonging to their own family and species. Not too close together, give room! Spread out over the land to give all equally good chances for breeding and feeding and the survival of each homesteading pair, give room!

Thousands upon thousands of various animate and inanimate parts compose these forest communities, one bounding on the next, one within the other. All are separate units, yet knit together in an astonishingly intricate web. Each part fits precisely into its designated compartment, effectively supporting, maintaining, and in one way or the other contributing to the

40

existence and the well-being of every other part and to the interrelated, the optimum, balance of all the systems.

❦

The time a woodpecker spends on the excavation of its nest cavity varies considerably from species to species. Much depends on the condition of the wood, the degree of core rot, whether the tree is dead or alive. The quality of the tool the woodpecker has evolved, the construction of its cranium and its bill, are also important. The excavation time is also influenced by the amount of distracting outside disturbances that affect the pair, and by the facility with which they achieve the required degree of compatible and effective interrelations. For example, the hairy woodpeckers, nesting early before the main flocks of the migrants arrive, prefer to bore their nests in live trees. Having to work in hard wood, they take from twenty-eight to thirty days to complete their cavity. The yellow-shafted flickers and the downy woodpeckers, boring their cavities in dead boles or choosing old holes, accomplish their nest preparations in twenty-one to twenty-two days.

As to Mar, after spending about one-third (to the female's one-tenth) of the daytime hours labouring on the nest for twenty-six days, his interest begins to lag. The enthusiasm and the tenacity with which he worked all this time weaken gradually as the hour draws nearer for the change that is scheduled to take place next. Once again the rhythms of the sapsuckers' life are due to change. To accommodate the new activities which soon are to occupy most of the birds' attention their habitual schedule must be adjusted. A smooth change-over keeps the whole system working at peak efficiency.

Now Mar spends most of his time just sitting with his feet gathered under him in the entrance of the nest cavity. He has hewn the opening to the exact measure of his sleek body with not

41

a millimetre to spare. With his red crest on end and the red bib under his chin ruffed, he sits there framed in the doorway. No one can get past him, his home is a fast fortress. Occasionally he disappears inside. Then, as often as not, driven by a last fling of hole-boring impulse, he chisels away a few more chips from the already perfectly formed cavity, slightly enlarging it. Some of the chips he lets fall on the floor, a mat of sawdust, others he gathers in his bill and with a desultory shake of his head he scatters them from the doorway.

Suddenly the female sweeps into sight. A soft chatter affirms the partners' keen awareness of each other. Instantly Mar springs to life. Aside indolence, aside lethargy! With a fine upward swing the female alights on the horizontal branch of the great white pine next to the nest tree. She struts and her movements suggest a special mission, a special meaning in the manner in which she presents herself. She adjusts herself crosswise on the branch. There she waits. Only a slight quiver of the red tip of her crest records the agitation that obviously consumes her.

Mar is not slow in responding. On wings beating fast between puffed shoulders in a grossly stilted way Mar darts from the nest. He flings himself sideways on to the horizontal branch a little distance from the female. The glint in his eye, the swagger of his movements, eloquently convey the mood that possesses him. He rights himself. Across the four or five feet that separate him from the female he makes his grandiose approach, tail trailing, back deeply depressed, bobbing, bill stabbing right and left. The sexual conqueror advances in all his glory.

The female crouches, she lifts her tail and her bill. And then she receives him in full conjugal capitulation. For a second Mar tramples lightly upon her back to make sure of his balance, then swings his whole body crosswise under her tail. For slightly more than ten seconds they are clasped together, Mar's left wing spread and seeking the support of the branch. Their pose is airy, ethereal, enchanting in the artless spontaneity of the moment.

42

Quickly they fly apart, Mar to the nest hole where he sits looking out. The female preens. Soon she is entirely absorbed in this agreeable occupation. She picks carefully through her feathers, one by one. Luxuriously she stretches one leg along an extended right wing.

This crowning period of their courtship activities continues over a span of about two weeks. During this time wild moments of tense sexual excitation alternate with many interruptions devoted to preening or to feeding, when the birds hungrily sidle along bands of opened sapwells, sipping sap, or they crawl along thin twigs high up in the leafy crowns of the trees, lapping the residual drops of sweet sap from springtime's overflowing rivulets; or they hunt swarming ants crawling on the ground. By the end of the first week their enthusiasm reaches its climax and the scales tip strongly in favour of almost continuous sexual stimulation and activities. At this stage a subtle interplay of intimately balanced reciprocation directs every move and pose, granting the initiative now to the male, now to the female. And the impact exercised by events and circumstances and their own attitudes toward each other govern all their moods and urgencies.

Almost imperceptibly an increasing broodiness takes possession of the female. A new change imposes itself upon the pattern of the birds' behaviour—as inevitably it must. And in keeping with the rising demands of these other impulses for greater attention, their sexual glow starts to decline. But although its final extinction is not really due until far into the next phase of the behavioural sequences, because of a very special event the female's mood changes first and she begins to reject Mar's courting advances.

❀

The time is a minute or two before sunrise. The female arrives, and she swoops up to the nest, eager and insistent. She wants in.

43

She pops her head inside several times before Mar answers her signal, and quickly she hops aside to let him out. The cavity is hers. She enters. She bides her time.

For an hour and ten minutes no outward sign betrays to me the existence of any life within the gaping hole. I all but miss the fleeting instant when, quick as a flash, she slips out and is gone. Only from later events am I able to prove that when she flew out she left an egg, gleaming white, on the bottom of the cavity.

Not long after her departure Mar returned. And at that moment, when on his way down he clung spreadeagled on the walls of the cavity, he must have seen the egg lying there innocently in the semi-darkness of the nest. The short time he remained invisible, he could hardly have achieved more than just turn around before he came out again. And there he sat now with his head framed in the doorway, watchful and alert.

Five days — five eggs! In the course of these signal five days Mar and the female visited the nest by turns. They came more frequently now than before and stayed longer, most often sitting in the doorway, watching, close to the eggs. Sometimes, when they disappeared inside for a short while, it is quite possible that they warmed the eggs briefly under their soft fluffed feathers.

Soon the sapsuckers began to prolong the brooding sessions. When they arrived at the nest, they no longer spent much time sitting looking out, but disappeared inside. Then their visits started to run into one another and the attending bird did not leave until the other one came to relieve it every half hour or so. From the day when this happened the sapsuckers began to incubate the eggs full time. By calculating the total time the birds were inside out of sight, together with the long nights Mar always slept in the nest, I was able to deduct that the two birds covered the eggs by turns no less than ninety-eight per cent of the twenty-four hours.

The yellow-shafted flickers as well as the hairy and the downy woodpeckers undergo the same change in behaviour as do the sapsuckers which indicates the conversion from egglaying to fulltime incubation. From then on the rhythm of the birds' daily activities acquires a different character. By starting his count from this day, the keen observer is able to obtain a fairly good idea of the length of the incubation periods of respective species.

This intermission in the lives of the sapsuckers descends upon them as one of profound quietude and relaxation. It is a time of rest and recuperation from the preceding stressful period of intensive territorial activities and courtship, a natural development in the succession of a well-balanced arrangement of events. Now the comings and goings of the pair are unproclaimed and secretive. Ostentation is muted and all their behaviour tends toward the small movements and noiselessness in the interest of concealment and nest security.

Once established, this rhythm is then set for the duration of this important section of the nesting cycle. Any disturbance heralds the happening of some untoward event. The glimpse of a predator, anything that is a threat to the safety of the nest instantly throws the routines of the sapsuckers out of kilter. And unless luck is with them, unless the birds are constantly watchful, ceaselessly on the defensive, such events might well presage an unsuccessful ending of the nesting.

Yet ritualistic movements and symbolic demonstrations persist even under these circumstances and are rigidly observed in all their details. The ceremonies during the incubation period are, in fact, a quaint mixture of the rituals performed during excavation, although in selection and execution some parts may be left out and others added. Softly murmured mewing notes give the relieving partner clearance to approach the nest unchallenged. The relief clings to the doorway, flicks its head from side to side across the opening. The moving shadow on the inside wall of the passage into the nest signals the arrival of relief. The sitting bird bursts through the opening, thrusting the relieving partner aside, and is gone.

45

There follows a curiously modified version of the ritual tapping ceremony, the same in essence as the birds performed when they met at the nest during excavation. Before entering, the relieving bird now taps at the lower edge of the doorway, adopting the same ceremonial pose and stilted movements as in the ritual tapping ceremony. At this time, however, the roles are reversed and the sequence slightly garbled: not the bird at the nest but the one that arrives taps, and this it does not as the mate arrives but after it has departed. Obviously, every part of it is highly meaningful and necessary in order to elicit from the pair the proper mutual responses. Probably the sudden proximity of the mate and the explosive exit of the one in the nest produce tensions that need to be thus dispelled. This ritual is omitted only when the incubating partner for some reason has left the nest before the relief arrives. I often speculated on how the birds knew when the nest was empty and when it was not? Did the pair meet, unknown to me? Did they catch a glimpse of each other that I missed?

❦

Around the nest all is quiet and peaceful. Mar is dozing on the eggs. Within the cavity he reacts by ear to what is going on outside, but takes no heed otherwise. After the female had covered the eggs for forty-four minutes—toward the end of the incubation period the sessions on the eggs are prolonged by about fifteen minutes—Mar had relieved her. Now she is off at last on her regular recess to feed and to preen and to rest.

The range is hers, she is in charge. She takes a keen interest in all that takes place around her. A great commotion arises in the northwest corner and she is irresistibly drawn towards it. Curiosity is a mighty impulse.

A gathering of small birds has assembled there. They utter sharp staccato notes, repeating them, thus giving vent to their

46

alarm, their fright, their anger. In their midst sits perched on a stout branch a large silent bird. It is a broad-winged hawk, loose of feather, short tail broadly barred. The hawk shows no interest in the throng of angry small birds; it is bored. The longer the harassment lasts, the more intense the excitement of the midgets. They dart at the hawk, quickly turning tail with loud cries, a marvellous game of derring-do. Sometimes the wind from the wings of the bravest ruffles the hawk's feathers, but not its haughty pose nor its temper. A highly safe game it is, this small birds' mobbing of the big hawk, a symbolic demonstration of the respective roles they are created to play in relation to each other in the great drama of life and nature.

The sapsucker female reacts to the hawk in her own specific way. She flies from one tree trunk to the next. She hides behind them, peering forth cautiously and uttering plaintive mewing notes. The hawk's tolerance is determined by its hunger and its disposition, and this in turn decides the duration of the mobbing. At last, unperturbed and unhurried, the hawk launches itself upon the air; its ample rounded wings flap heavily. And left behind is a throng of small birds, seemingly unaware of the departure, still protesting the danger that is no longer there. Eventually the lack of stimulation by sight and sound abates their tempers. One by one they drop off absorbed once again in their own private affairs.

Now Mar has flown and the female is in the nest. Peacefully she sits on the eggs. The minutes pass. Mar is due to return soon. She hears his soft mewing notes signalling his arrival, she crawls to the doorway and sits there, looking out. Mar alights a foot from the entrance. At that moment the red squirrel runs down its stub. Mar dashes away. He stalks the squirrel at a discreet distance, hiding behind the tree trunks. On an errand of her own, the squirrel runs too close to Mar's tree. Mar darts to the doorway, but the female bars the entrance. Frantically he tries to push his way in to defend the young. The female regards him as an

47

enemy and her sharp jabbing bill sends him flying.

❀

Springtime blends into summer. The days are warmer and the sunshine richer. Tepid showers wet the lush verdure of sprouting ferns, jewelweeds, aster leaves and honeysuckle. Heavy drops of water accumulate, fall, and like transparent pearls roll off the green leaves that intercept their downfall. And where they fall the earth greedily soaks them up. The humidity of the air stands like vapour amongst the trees, and for a short while the crisp northern forest takes on the hot moist atmosphere of its tropical counterpart. Mosquitoes, mysteriously sensing the presence of mammalian blood, buzz plaintively. Swarms of black flies rise from the forest floor where mosses and earth are disturbed. And with legendary patience the snowshoe hare lifts a quick paw to wipe a blood-ripe tick off its nose, one of dozens that fastened itself upon the hare's long-suffering hide as the animal brushed past the insects' hiding place.

The female is on the nest. It is hot and she feels the need for relief. She crawls to the doorway, and I see her sitting there with her bill open, panting, ventilating away from her the heat. All the feathers on her head and body are smoothed down, diminishing their insulating propensity to a minimum. Pushing with her feet from behind and giving herself added propulsion by the lever action of the top of her head against the upper edge of the doorway, she squeezes through the opening. She swings out her tail and clings listlessly to the warm trunk. She is utterly relaxed, indolent from the heat, yet keenly alert to every sound that reaches her feather-covered ears. And the way she grasps their portent is partly innate, partly learned, an ability sharpened by habit, by her familiarity with the territorial scene.

She goes back in again, and soft tapping sounds come from within, muted as they were during the excavation period. She

48

comes to the doorway with her bill full of chips. With a shake of the head she scatters them, and slowly they drift to the ground upon the still air. She repeats this maneuvre several times, presumably slightly enlarging the room inside.

On the last occasion she emerges and lingers in the doorway. But the relieving mate is still not in sight. Mar's absences have lengthened noticeably during the past few days. No longer does his prompt arrival after nicely regulated intervals herald her release from duty. She gives up waiting and withdraws again inside.

The thirteenth day of the sapsuckers' slow-motion incubation period dawns. The female may not be aware that one of the eggs under her is pipped. Something inside began to tap upon the encasing wall and to push weakly against it. The faint sounds of the emerging, peeping chick, the surreptitious activity going on under her, gradually infiltrate the female's awareness.

When they do, she rises. I can see the shadow of her head playing faintly on the walls leading down into the cavity. At that very moment the pipping may actually have encircled the large end of the egg and it falls apart. Out rolls a naked, wrinkle-skinned, pulsing warm thing against the female's own denuded breast. She feels the physical contact with her progeny. She crawls to the doorway and without waiting for relief flies away.

Soon she is back, and she has a tiny mite clasped in her bill, proof absolute of the great event that is currently taking place in the sapsuckers' nest. At least one of the eggs has released from its shelter a sapsucker hatchling. Ever so lightly the female's bill touches the swollen, highly sensitive corners of the nestling's mouth. It springs open to receive for the first time an offering of extra-ovular food that slowly slides down the worm-like neck.

❁

The end of a period, the beginning of another; one phase blends into the next, not always perfectly smoothly but quite inexorably. And to watch the manner in which these adjustments are carried out, this refitting of habits and behaviour into the new framework to suit the demands of an entirely altered situation with immutable natural logic and consequence, is the most fascinating in the study of nature.

# Chapter Five

## The Gift of Life

**M**ar backed down the trunk of the red pine, quickly, sideways to the left, then to the right, half spiralling, casting a cautious eye behind him to see where he was going. Hopping directly downwards on a tree trunk, as the nuthatches do with supreme assurance, is an art that somehow has escaped the sapsuckers as well as all other woodpeckers. Mar's half slithering sideways locomotion caused his scratching claws to dislodge small, reddish pieces of bark that fell to the ground.

Below, a trickling rivulet formed a miniature backwater pool that lies gleaming in the sunlight. This is Mar's goal. On the ground he hops across the bed of warm, redolent pine needles on to the green moss. He bends down and drinks deeply from the pool, for it is a hot day.

Lovely cool water, moving glittering water! The sight allures and he hops right into it. His wings beat the water into a cascade of sparkling drops. He gets soaked and just sits there for thirty long seconds, half immersed, motionless in the middle of the pool. The look in his eye and his languid pose betray his sensation of vast enjoyment.

Finally he leaves the pool and flies back to the pine. His

beating wings create a fine spray that envelops him in a shower of glittering drops. He hops up the trunk of the pine. The remaining water caught in his feathers runs off his tail, leaving a dark wet trail all the way. By the time he is ready to take off for home every part of his well-oiled plumage appears to be bone-dry.

Mar flies to the nest and, according to habit deeply ingrained since the first day of incubation, he alights in the tree standing at a distance from the nest to survey the situation. At that moment he is fully aware that the female is absent. With a long, deep sweep he alights at the doorway and, omitting the shift ritual, quickly vanishes within.

This is Mar's first visit to the nest after the hatching of the eggs began. His speedy reappearance from inside informs me that the signal event has not escaped his cognizance. And, as if to give me further proof that young are in the nest, he carries in his bill a small package of excreta neatly wrapped in a thin transparent membrane and rolled in sawdust.

In a highly ritualized moth-like flight Mar transports the tiny package to a tree thirty feet from the nest and carefully deposits it in a crevice of the ridged bark; whereupon he wipes his bill thoroughly. This ceremony is performed every time the nest needs cleaning. When the young leave four weeks later, the tree is festooned with desiccated packages and a litter of others lie fertilizing the ground beneath. Thus each ceremony, each ritualistic movement performed by the sapsuckers, marks with its own distinctive symbolism the particular behaviour pattern it has been created to embellish and lends to it special emphasis and meaning.

❁

Spontaneously and effortlessly Mar and his female fall into the new routine required by the new life within the cavity. They continue to brood the nestlings for a time, but their sessions are now interrupted by feedings. Gradually, the direct shifts with their accompanying ceremony are neglected. As the nestlings grow and develop, the shifts cease altogether and the pace of activities increases.

When the young birds reach the age of five days, the sapsuckers begin activities a few minutes before sunrise. Their day of labour lasts until soon after sunset, a total of seventeen hours and fifteen minutes. Three-quarters of this time the parents spend warming the chicks, sharing almost equally in this task. They collect and carry to the nestlings 127 meals at the rate of $7^1/2$ feedings an hour. Of these, Mar brings half as many more than the female does, and his offerings are noticeably larger. Thus, supposing there are four nestlings at this time and they are being fed one at a time, each of them received not quite two meals every hour.

The male's role in the family affairs of the sapsuckers, and indeed also in that of the other woodpeckers mentioned earlier, is an interesting one. It is he who stakes out the territory and endows it with his conspicuous presence. It is he who for the most part chooses the site of the nest. Only under special circumstances does the female sapsucker carry through her selection, as, for instance, when she returns to the territory where she nested last year and finds herself without a male. With a new mate, acquired later, the pair remain there to nest. The downy is the only species of woodpeckers among those I know in which the female's choice of nest site may prevail more often than the male's. The male sapsucker also performs the major part of the excavation of the cavity. Indeed, the female hardly takes any part at all except at the very last, although this, too, may vary individually.

Within two realms, the egglaying and the incubation, the female reigns supreme. In the first one she is essential and this, to some extent, carries over into the next phase, when during the daytime she exhibits an impulse to brood more predominant than the male's. But then again, after this period is over, the male sapsucker is once more ready to take upon himself the lion's share of the care of the young, their feeding and the sanitation of the nest. And it is now during this significant part of the nesting that the remarkable flexibility and sensitivity of parental responses, this built-in tendency to react in a compensatory manner, comes to the fore. Again it is the male that displays these attributes most prominently. Without them, the prognosis of the nesting success might well be placed in jeopardy. At any stage of the nesting cycle the female sapsucker appears incapable of redeeming the loss of the male. His is a life of consequence.

❦

Now it's midsummer—the sun is reaching its highest point in the heavens, and the days are stretching their allotted minutes to reach their longest duration, before the sun, once again, begins its reverse movement southward.

Now it's summer—blossom time is already past and the fertilized pistils are swelling into ripening, luscious fruits. Already the leaves of the trees have lost the freshness of their light green spring colour and are changing into the darker hues of maturity. Like a sea of tall green umbrellas stands the bracken, protecting the forest floor from midsummer's strong sunbeams and hiding living things in safe places out of sight beneath its spreading canopy.

Now it's summer—the ants are swarming on frail transparent wings. And suddenly the ants are down on the sun-hot ground, looking irritable and desperate, exposed to the insectivorous predators, of which the sapsucker is one. And after the swarming of the ants, other insects enter upon their brief episodes of ecstasy, dancing in small groups in the air, up and down in light graceful movements, up and down, without effort, without purpose it seems, light ephemeral beings absorbed in the fulfilment of their destinies.

Now it's summer—the mayflies appear, rising as if by a miracle from the water of the lake. They are the most elegant of midsummer's creatures with their curved bodies and gossamer wings, with their two sensitive antennae adorning their heads and the long hair-fine fibrils sprouting from their posteriors. High and low they dance, filling every space between the forest trees, up and down, opening and closing their intricate figures, a concentrated airy biomass, dancing endlessly into the dusk, into the shining moonlight.

And after the mayflies' night of triumph, in the morning every branch, every leaf, every surface, is plastered with them, their tails with the long twin hairs still jauntily curved upwards. But the energy that buoyed them during their day's and their night's dancing has deserted them. They sit inert as if glued to their support. And only an errant current of air gently stirs their tailend adornments.

For a week, each day new swarms of mayflies rise from the tepid shallows of the lake, thousands that in their latter stages of development have escaped the mass of fishes that prey upon them. Then they dance their nuptial dance, their brief moment of existence and ecstasy, their life, their very animation, bought at the price of death, as is the logical fulfilment that awaits every living thing.

The timing of the nestlings' appearance in the sapsuckers' cavity and the first stage of their development coincide with the swarming of the ants and the mayflies, insects eminently suitable in size for the young birds. The great abundance of easily picked food stimulates the sapsuckers' foraging urge. They alight in the midst of the bonanza and gorge upon the insects, then cram their bills full. By the time the parent reaches home, the load it carries is partially crushed into a rich pulp. Mouths open like pink blossoms on swaying stems. Quickly the parent shoves its gift of food down the throat of the strongest, the most pushy of the nestlings.

The nestlings develop comparatively rapidly during the first two weeks, gaining steadily in weight. The eagerness with which their gaping beaks shoot up to greet the parent as it darkens the doorway attests to their increasing demand for more food. The soft chatter they utter almost continuously except when asleep, the nestlings' means of communicating with parents and siblings, grows louder. And all this stimulates the parents' feeding response. Day by day they increase the feeding rate. By the time the nestlings are thirteen to fourteen days old, their parents are crowding seventeen feedings into the hour, providing a nestful of four young with slightly more than four meals an hour.

By this time the parents cease brooding the young by day. They haven't got time. Whether Mar covers them at night or just sleeps clinging to the wall of the cavity probably depends on circumstances. The days and the nights are warm now and, besides, as their warm insulating feathers grow out, the nestlings gradually acquire thermostatic control. Therefore, the feeding of the progeny is uppermost on the parents' agenda at this time and they establish a highly efficient shuttle service, well timed and well balanced.

The sapsuckers' day begins at a comparatively slow pace, because after the night's fast the birds emerge hungry and feeding takes precedence above all else. About midday the parents have another good meal themselves, and a third in the afternoon. Meanwhile, they gradually increase the feeding rate of the young until it reaches a peak for the day one or two hours before time comes to go to roost. The whole family goes to sleep well fed.

The increased feeding rate and only one nestling being fed at each visit necessitates a rapid routine—in, feed, out—which takes less than a minute. This activity is at times so fast, breathless is an appropriate description, that the observer is sometimes left wondering if it did, in fact, take place. Add to this the task of cleaning up the nest, which involves picking up a fecal sac, carrying it out and depositing it on the rough-barked tree, and it is quite evident that the labours attached to raising a sapsucker family entail not only dexterity and skill in finding the food, but stamina and sedulity as well.

The faster feeding schedule excludes too many long intervals between the feedings and, in consequence, the shorter intervals, lasting from one to eight minutes, increase. This cuts down the time left for the parents to feed themselves, to preen and to rest. Quite naturally this intensifies their nervous tension. It also makes them more sensitive to the events that take place in the environment, and ultimately this causes disturbances in the feeding schedule. In fact, the slightest impediment obstructing the sapsuckers' efforts to maintain the increased pace in and out of the nest elicits significant reactions in their behaviour.

With the faster clip of feeding, for one thing, the parents chance to meet more frequently at the nest. This upsets them, for they cannot go in and feed the young both at the same time. So they fly away without feeding. The female, whose urge to feed is weaker than the male's, usually swallows the food she brought, or carries it away and drops it. Only later, after she has collected another load, she returns, and the nestlings miss a meal. Mar, whose feeding drive is stronger, also flies away with the food, but he returns almost immediately and, if all is well, goes in to feed. Not surprisingly, all this adds to the nervous tensions of the parents.

The faster feeding schedule also brings about greater commotion around the nest tree and robs it of much of its seal of secrecy. This, in turn, leads visitors and predators to evince more interest in it, so it requires intensified defence. Naturally, the result is a lowering of the sapsuckers' threshold for tolerance of intruders. And the female, who has more time at her disposal because of a less demanding feeding schedule, takes upon herself the more active role of chasing uninvited visitors away, while Mar, ever on the alert, blocks the doorway.

One day the neighbouring sapsucker female crosses the unde-

57

fined border between the areas of mine and thine, intent on finding food for her young in the nest. Mar's female catches sight of her. She engages the intruder in a lively aggressive display, wings flicking, bill pointing right and left. This throws Mar into a passion of excitement—probably because the altercation takes place so close to the nest. He dashes out to join in the display, but, true to his prevailing impulse to protect the nest, dashes back in again. In this way he continues to dart in and out several times. Exaggerated behaviour of this kind shows overpowering excitement. Excitement is always contagious. It has a stimulating effect on Mar's female. Instantly she darts at the intruder, forcibly dislodging her, and the chase is on out of sight.

When the female returns, excitation still ruffles Mar's sensibilities. He attacks her, uttering sharp notes. But, clinging to the branch and giving soft mewing notes, her plumage smoothed down making her look very thin, she adopts a submissive attitude. And once again friendly relations between them are restored.

The pileated woodpecker is as large as a crow and has exciting black, white and red colouring. The male with his flamboyant scarlet crest and with a noisily begging fledgling in tow alights on the red squirrel's stub close to the sapsuckers' nest tree. This causes sudden and overwhelming consternation in the sapsuckers' camp. Defiant of danger, they dash at the two large woodpeckers in a kind of joint fly-past attack aimed at dislodging the giant enemies. But the pileated woodpeckers show no sign of even seeing the midget attackers. Highly exaggerated stimuli release exaggerated reactions. Prey to intense nervous stress, therefore, the sapsuckers alight on a nearby branch and there, in a burst of redirected motivation, they embark upon a prolonged and animated aggressive display against each other. By the time they finally return to their senses, the pileated woodpeckers have long since slipped out of sight.

Nervous tension and stress act like power units that release new bursts of energy into the living system. This is the animation of life. It pushes the organism from one situation to the next, from struggle to rest, and forward to meet new demands upon its powers of adjustment, of adaptability, of grasping and assimilating new versatilities. In the sapsuckers these constant stressful interruptions in their daily routines quite naturally affect the set schedules, in particular their feeding rates. As a result, a reduction in the growth rate of the nestlings is unavoidable.

Long since the nestlings' eyes have opened and their plumage, save for their tails, has grown out almost completely, covering them well. The young are becoming more active. They are beginning to cling to the walls of the cavity, impetuously intercepting the food-bearing parent in the short corridor between the cavity itself and the doorway. The female whose feeding impulse is not geared very high reacts strongly to the new set-up. She arrives at the nest and pops her head inside. But when she finds herself unexpectedly confronting the advancing nestling, she turns tail and flies off without delivering her meal.

This tantalizing behaviour only adds to the nestlings' excitement. They want food. They crawl farther and farther up toward the doorway. They fight among themselves for the front spot.

Mar overcomes the shock of the new set-up with greater facility, partly because his feeding drive continues to be comparatively strong, and he quickly adjusts to the new situation. Starting by going in so far that only the tip of his tail shows in the opening and then backing out, he feeds his active progeny. And then gradually, by stages within the next day or so, the nestlings force him back, or rather out, until he is finally obliged to feed them clinging to the doorway outside.

Occasionally the impulse to clean out the nest gets the better of him. In a burst of energy he pushes the nestful of would-be fledglings right back to the bottom of the cavity. Half a second later he emerges with an enormous load of sawdust-wrapped droppings which he, with due ceremony and care, deposits on the trunk of the rough-barked tree.

By this time the combined number of feedings per hour have declined to about half their peak frequency. Even Mar's feeding rate drops sharply, but he compensates for this to some extent by bringing much larger meals than previously. These meals consist mainly of large moths, especially the forest tent caterpillar moths which ravage these northern forests in recurring cycles, and hard-bodied beetles. The latter require a certain amount of preparation before they are fit to be fed to the nestlings. Banging the load against a branch or trunk, Mar often spends up to four minutes mashing the feedings into a rough pulp before he takes them to the doorway to pop down the waiting nestling's throat.

Meanwhile, the female, having at last reconciled herself to the new practice of feeding the young from the outside, is less particular about bringing food regularly. As usual she catches smaller insects. Therefore, the decline of her working schedule is neither so noticeable nor so abrupt as the male's.

One can feel it in the air. One can observe the effect of it upon the parents. The time of the significant event is approaching, the time when the young sapsuckers are preparing to leave the natal cavity. Once again the nervous tensions mount.

There is also another reason for the renewed excitement. With the first nesting cycle drawing to a close a new mood awakens within the adult sapsuckers. There is a revival of their reproductive behaviour. They begin to fly about in the same fashion as they did in the spring when territorial affairs took up so much of their time and energies. They neglect the young ones in the nest. They drum prolonged resonant tattoos, an exercise almost forgotten since they became totally occupied with incubating the eggs. They meet in exciting courtship displays once again, and dart away giving their come-hither flightsongs.

The young ones sit in the doorway and watch the antics of the adults. They want food. And the excitement grows in the young ones as well as in the adults. And all of this serves to create in all of them the appropriate mood.

The nestlings take turns sitting in the doorway. The sound of their nearly unceasing chatter pulsates through the forest in the midsummer heat. They look out upon an enticing yet forbidding new world with great interest. They begin to react to every event outside. A parental warning note immobilizes them in petrified silence. A fly buzzing in the doorway releases wild awkward efforts to capture it. A thunderclap sends them precipitately to the bottom of the cavity, not to betray their existence until peace and tranquility warrant their safe reappearance in the doorway. Every glimpse they catch of a neglectful parent, or the sight at long last of one approaching with food, arouses an excitation within the nest that knows no bounds.

And thus dawns the twenty-sixth day in the life of Mar's almost full-fledged brood.

# Chapter Six

## The First Flight

It was cool when I came out in the morning on the twenty-sixth day after the young hatched. Fine droplets of dew covered every leaf and adhered like strings of minute pearls to every thread of cobweb. A thrush, a tawny veery, was engaged in a lyric performance of rare musicality, a flow of silvery dulcet notes in a descending cadence leisurely repeated over and over again. The epilogue of a successful nesting season was never more beautifully expressed. In the voluminous crown of a tall birch the ever-present red-eyed vireo moved about collecting food for a late brood hatched at last after other attempts to nest ended in disaster, all the while uttering its short songs, slightly varied in composition, of clear rounded notes.

In the sapsuckers' nest the young ones were noisy, though for the moment out of sight down at the bottom of the cavity. Soft mewing notes announced Mar's pending arrival with his bill full of food. The faint noise he made brought the nestlings scrambling up from the depths. As the food-bearing parent approached closer, the welcoming chatter swelled into a mighty chorus.

One nestling pushes its way to the foremost position in the doorway. A suffused ashy-brown colour, lighter on the breast, covers its front parts. Two dull white lines run along each of its cheeks, the forerunners of the distinctive white markings that are later to adorn the mature bird's head. The erected crest is tinted pink and a pinkish spot, the bud of the coming red throat patch, tells me that the young bird is a male. The father clings to the doorway and quickly fills the son's gullet with food, nearly choking him. The operation distorts the young bird's juvenile chatter into a weird scream.

Hastily Mar departs. And the young one as if intent upon following the father squeezes far out through the doorway. This is it! I hold my breath. But in the last instant the nestling withdraws and thus saves itself from an unexpected tumble into the outside world. It was a narrow escape. For a while the nestling just sits there, gazing after the departing parent with an expression of keen interest.

A short while later both parents are back near the nest. Rousing movements take place in front of the nestling's eyes. The adults fly about; they make no attempt to approach nest and nestling. Suddenly they engage in a full courtship display, facing each other, bills high swinging right and left, backs depressed, tails trailing and wings flicking gently. They ignore the nest, ignore the nestling, ignore everything except each other. They fly apart. The next instant they cling each to a tree trunk, resting and preening, intent upon their own comfort and well-being as if the nestlings did not exist, as if their chatter could not be heard.

This parental behaviour tantalizes the young sapsuckers. Excitedly they move about behind the doorway, they change places, fight among themselves. But the parents hear nothing, see nothing. As the adult sapsuckers in the course of these various movements approach or draw away from the nest, the nestlings' chatter increases in volume or wanes, like the noise of the surf upon the beach.

Soon the increasing excitation gets the better of all of them. The nestling out front tentatively, impatiently squeezes in and out of the doorway. Every so often it almost—but never quite—topples through the opening. Miraculously it recovers its balance to pop back in again safely.

This state of affairs continues all morning. As usual the female sapsucker shows the greatest uneasiness over this break in the set routine. The nestlings' remarkable vivacity intimidates her. As a result her feeding rate registers a spectacular drop. Why is this? Obviously, the time for the nestlings' emergence from the nest is fast approaching. Perhaps this is a kind of adaptive behaviour on the part of the parents, serving to encourage the young ones to leave the safe shelter of the nest, to make the significant drop into the outside world, entrusting themselves to nothing but the support of a pair of untried wings?

Following his never-failing impulse to make up for the female's neglect, Mar continues to bring meals to the nestlings, although neither so regularly nor so often as he did yesterday. This means that for some time the young ones are being kept at a marginal level of hunger. So naturally they now react more intensely to the sight and movements of the parents which, in turn, intensifies the parents' excitement. All this demonstrates the constant mutual interplay between the male and the female, and between parental and filial responses. And the effect is the rising excitation of the participants, which will eventually bring about the signal event of nest-leaving.

This change in the parents' behaviour occurred well ahead of the actual hour of emergence in slightly varying forms in all the woodpeckers. The parents' seeming neglect in combination with a drastically lowered rate of feeding from that of the earlier part of the nestlife, inevitably had the effect of keeping the nestlings below the normal level of satiety. As their hunger increased, the nestlings' frustration at having to wait so long for every mouthful of food added mightily to their growing excitement. They expressed their impatience and their impetuosity by vociferous calling and by indulging in lively exercises of squeezing in and out of the doorway.

The premature occurrence of these exciting events once contributed to the emergence a few days earlier than scheduled of a brood of still stubby-tailed flickers. Their nest hole was an old one used many years before, enlarged and thin-walled from wear and with a generously dimensioned doorway. This allowed the growing nestlings plenty of room to play and to cavort together inside. It also gave them an early opportunity to become acquainted with the outside world and to observe the comings and goings of their parents. These were strong stimuli indeed. Little wonder then that their precocious behaviour brought about a reaction of pre-emergence neglect in the parents. And this, of course, caused the young flickers to leave the nest too soon.

On another occasion, a brood of downy woodpecker nestlings so strenuously objected to the parents' missed-meal tactics that they actually fought the father when he came to feed them. They bit and pulled at the father's breast feathers while their mother kept well out of reach. When she came with food at last, they attacked her and she flew away without feeding any of them. Then again when the father came with food, one of the hungry youngsters charged him with such vigour that it overshot the limit of safe return. Undismayed the fledgling swung its whole body out tail first and then staged a hitching pursuit in dizzy circles around the trunk of the nest stub after the startled and hastily retreating father, finally forcing him to yield the coveted meal.

❀

Now a daughter sits in the doorway of Mar's nest. Like her brother, she has that ashy-brown colouring over head, neck and shoulders, that provides such fine protecting camouflage for the young sapsuckers. The front part of her crest is dull pink like her brother's, the initial hue that with maturity is to turn into scarlet. Unlike the brother, the daughter's throat patch is pure white with a fringe of white dots along the lower edge, the pearly attribute of female juvenility.

The young bird is a lively one. Eagerly she pops out at the doorway, then back in. Her bright eyes follow everything that goes on outside. She twists her head and gazes inquisitively in various directions. She pecks vigorously on the upper edge of the doorway, and then on the lower edge. The special tempo of this pecking and the tilt of her head recall the ritual tapping ceremony, this important part of the sapsucker's adult behaviour pattern that will come to play so significant a role in her own reproductive life, especially during the excavation period. How often is not adult behaviour reproduced, or perhaps initiated, early in life in this reflected fashion, as if to prepare through practice the young animal for later behavioural phases of particular significance!

Extreme excitation grips the young daughter at times. But at the moment the parents are absent and her emotional stress obviously is not caused by outside stimuli. She pushes herself far out through the opening. She is going to topple out into the awaiting world! But as always, these daring exercises are nothing but make-believe. She pops back in again and is unceremoniously replaced in the doorway by another daughter.

The parents continue to feed the young ones very irregularly. Mar, still the more solicitous of the two parents, succeeds in keeping the nestlings from suffering actual hunger by bringing them food as it suits him at rather protracted intervals.

Suddenly the neighbouring red squirrel enters upon the scene uninvited quite close to Mar's nest tree, scolding loudly. Mar dashes headlong into the doorway. But there, confrontation with the young ones crowding in the corridor unnerves him. He abandons his usual reaction to an enemy near the nest—taking up a strategic position inside the doorway with his sharp bill at the ready. Instead he pushes all the nestlings roughly back into the cavity. In the half darkness a collection of gleaming white drop-

67

pings stare him in the face, and his natural impulse to rid the nest of offal gets the better of him. The next instant—enemy or no enemy—he reappears with a load dripping from his bill. And once again I realize how easily and how aptly an entirely unrelated and redirected activity serves to relieve the pressure and the stress accumulating from a threatening situation.

In the same fluttering ceremonial flight as he always assumes when engaged in any important business that has to do with the nest, Mar transports the load of droppings to the disposal trunk and thoroughly wipes his bill afterwards. The squirrel has vanished; what Mar would have done had she still been there, I cannot even guess. Quickly he dashes back into the nest and reappears with another load that he deposits on the trunk with great ceremony. Twice more he does this in rapid succession. The breathless way in which he performs these activities suggests the compelling effect of the double stimuli to which he was being exposed—the threat of an enemy and the lamentable state of the cavity, together with his need for relief from the ensuing nervous tension.

In the early afternoon another son occupies the foremost position in the doorway of the nest, and Mar feeds him there. Intently watching the departing parent, while he enthusiastically pops out and in, the son suddenly reaches the point of no return. Untried wings spread automatically, and the young one is airborne. Wobbling, losing altitude, the fledgling falters, uncertain where to make a safe landing. But he makes it, about twelve feet down low on the trunk of a young pine. I feel robbed by the lack of drama with which the great event finally took place.

The son calls loudly. Mar hears the wail, takes one look at the precocious one. But this time the female quickly comes to the rescue and shoves the first meal down the new fledgling's eager throat.

Early the next morning the female, true to her habit, arrives at the nest calling gaily. Her bill is empty. The daughter pushes through the doorway in avid anticipation and grabs after the expected meal that is not there. The female flees. The daughter squeezes in and out several times with such vigour that suddenly her wings are released from the imprisonment of the nest hole and she is free. She flutters her wings desperately to keep aloft but sinks before her eager, strong claws reach out to grasp at the trunk of a birch ten feet away, hardly more than a foot from the ground.

If the daughter's first flight into the wide open world implied much faltering and inexperience, she needed no further lesson to hitch up the trunk of the birch to a respectable height in approved woodpecker fashion. She sees her father approaching. She greets him no longer with the infantile chatter she uttered while in the nest. Suddenly she has grown up and with that she has acquired her own newfangled version of the soft mewing notes with which her parents never miss to greet each other whenever they meet. The new situation of a daughter out of the nest calls for a change in Mar's behaviour also, for as he arrives with food he responds with a hoarse note not heard before.

Now the daughter's metamorphosis from nestling to fledgling progresses by leaps and bounds. Again she takes off, and though she is still uncertain of her bearings, this time she flies no less than sixty feet, concluding her triumphant course with an adult-like swoop high up on to the trunk of a tall aspen.

An hour later daughter number two, soon after followed by number three, leave the nest. The sapsuckers' whole brood are on the wing. The last fledgling is the weakest one, a victim of one of nature's manifold ways of adjusting the number of consumers to the available food resources. She negotiates her flight in an aimless, butterfly-like way; she wobbles and winds in and out of the undergrowth clipping the leaves with the tips of her uncertain wings, unable to gain altitude. At last, fluttering mightily, she manages to get sufficient lift under her wings to land eighteen feet above the level from which she took off.

The proficiency with which young woodpeckers make their first flight varies from one species to another. The surroundings of the nest, whether in a closed forest or in a more open place, and the degree of nestling development, are among the influencial factors. Thus the young downy woodpecker, emerging after only three weeks in the nest loses altitude on its first flight, but is agile or daring enough to betake itself farther than the sapsucker fledgling can. The hairy woodpecker fledgling, by contrast, stays in the nest slightly more than four weeks. On its first outing it is able to cover without any difficulty a considerable distance in a surprisingly powerful flight. And to this fledgling altitude presents no problem at all.

❦

A short while after the departure of the last nestling, Mar revisits the empty nest. But now no impetuous birdlings greet him with their rousing chatter. All is silence and emptiness. Mar hesitates. The unaccustomed situation does not fit the habit ingrained by long usage. The change requires from him an altered response. It takes him slightly by surprise; he is not ready for it.

For a full minute he clings to the doorway, looking in, weaving his head right and left across the opening. He enters; he stays inside for another full minute. Had I expected to see him coming out with a last load of droppings from the accumulation that surely must have been covering the floor of the cavity I am mistaken, for he flies out empty-billed.

I continue to wait for the conclusion of the last scene at the sapsuckers' abandoned nest site — if one is still to be enacted. This time I am not mistaken.

Once again Mar returns. How strong, how tenacious, are his ties with this old nest that his own indomitable efforts created, that held his clamorous progeny! This time his bill is full of food.

He pops halfway in through the doorway. But something aborts his obvious intention of entering. Quickly he retreats and flies away with all the food still clutched in the bill.

Time passes. Dusk settles softly around the end of the day. With some difficulty I discern a dim slender form making the usual approach by stages from tree to tree toward the nest. It is Mar. He calls softly, but no one answers. Once again he clings to the doorway worn smooth by long usage and looks in. He utters another soft call. But nothing answers his call. Emptiness, silence! It is nearly dark. Like a lost shadow Mar flies away.

Night falls. For the first time in fifty-two days Mar roosts outside and alone, clinging to the trunk of a dew-wet tree.

# Chapter Seven

## Restoring the Balance

The prolonged nest life period, necessary for the sapsucker nestlings to develop sufficiently before emerging from the nest, is for the parents a time of gradually mounting tension and stress. Day by day the demands of the nestlings increase, forcing upon the parents accelerating activities and expenditure of energy.

Naturally, increasing attendance upon the growing youngsters is bound to encroach upon the personal comforts of the parents. Less time is available to spend upon their own needs of feeding, resting and preening. Also, the loss of secrecy around the nest, caused by the parents' stepped up comings and goings and the nestling's swelling noisiness, requires sharper vigilance, and more energetic defence of the premises. So it is not hard to understand that, by the time the fledglings are about to burst forth upon the waiting world, the parents who raised them may be in a state of quite seriously sapped stamina and vitality.

The time allotted for this vital nest life is short and the demands upon the avian parent are great. An instance has been recorded of such exhaustion striking a pair of black-capped chickadees trying to raise a brood of eight that the parents' survival actually hung in the balance. In the case of Mar and his

73

female, the loss of one nestling (hatched from their original clutch of five eggs but never seen to emerge,) through their inability to provide sufficient nourishment for all, represents one of those necessary sacrifices nature frequently demands to ensure the survival of the rest of the brood. Often the mercy of nature is concealed under a cloak of apparent ruthlessness.

The pressure on the sapsucker parents diminished with the emergence of the four nestlings. Certainly, the youngsters still had to be fed, but attendance upon the free-flying fledglings needed to be neither so regular nor so frequent as when they were still in the nest. Moreover, the parents now shared the chore of feeding them more equally than before.

Loud, rather wheezy location notes, the juvenile version of the *oh-weee* call of the adults, are the primary means by which the new fledgling maintains its link with the family. The ear of the parent is finely attuned to these cries. They keep the parent well informed of the youngster's whereabouts and of the degree of its hunger.

The calling of the fledgling intensifies. Mar has his bill full of food. Even before he goes in search of his clamouring progeny he starts uttering loud notes in response. The young one listens. Reacting to the parental voice, it makes impatient movements. Its crest is erect, its wings flap lightly.

The next instant the fledgling catches sight of the parent. This excites the fledgling and its location notes change into mewing notes of recognition. The young one flaps its wings. It cannot wait. Hurry, hurry! Aggressively it jerks its head right and left. Even in the midst of this exciting coming together of parent and offspring, the fledgling is compelled by innate inclination to assert the zone of unapproachable individual distance between itself and all other creatures, if only as a token. The parent looks soft and friendly. The feathers on top of Mar's head and along his whole body are sleeked down, his eyes appear large and gleaming. He is shorn of all hostile attributes, and his bill is full of food. He infuses the fledgling with confidence.

The two birds meet on the trunk of a tree. Mar's offering of food immediately counteracts the fledgling's personal withdrawal. The crucial moment is upon them. Amid loud mutual vociferations, Mar delivers the bountiful meal deep down into the gullet of the convulsively swallowing fledgling. Mar flies off, and the young one is left, sitting there sated and relaxed for so long as the quiescent moment lasts.

Which one among the fledglings received the coveted meal depended largely upon which one cried the loudest and pursued the parent most energetically. Sometimes both parents reacted simultaneously to the come-hither signals of one fledgling. On these occasions the parents alighted on either side of the begging one to dispense in turn their gifts of food. Such double stimuli had the fledgling almost beside itself with excitement. Ostensibly, it found itself on the horns of a dilemma—to which parent ought it to address its most sedulous supplications to gain the largest offering of food?

The fledglings remain dependent on the support of the parents for varying lengths of time. The more precocious ones, having already started while in the nest to peck on their own, soon learn to recognize suitable food items and where to get them. They watch the parents feeding. This stimulates their desire to do likewise, a procedure the ethologists term sympathetic induction. At other times the young ones resort to the trial and error method. Within a week or ten days these advanced youngsters are quite capable of fending for themselves. Only one son and a daughter, a bit slower and more backward than the rest, continue to pursue the weary parents for another one or two weeks, until sharp and unfriendly nips from the parental bills finally succeed in repulsing them.

❁

Once again more or less on their own, certainly less distracted by the demanding concerns of family care, Mar and his mate now are able to indulge freely in their reawakened reproductive inclinations. They display—bobbing, flicking their wings. The young ones join, by sympathetic induction, in these exciting demonstrations to the edification of all of them. Thus they add to the rest yet another learning experience of movements and ritual which, less than a year hence, they will be destined to enact on their own behalf.

Quick responses to drumming signals, part and parcel of the sapsuckers' earlier territorial behaviour, every so often interrupt these displays. This serves me particularly well as I am able to follow them, to call them out, as I did in the spring. The day they fail to heed my imitation signals, when no tattoo, no call, no bird appears in response, I know that the ephemeral episode of their renewed courtship behaviour is drawing to a close.

Following the ardent nesting season as merely an afterthought, the sapsuckers' reproductive revival does not last more than two or three weeks. Though in these northern latitudes insufficient time prevents the sapsuckers from crowding another breeding cycle of seventy to seventy-five days into the short summer season, it safeguards nature's principle prevalent in all its unstinting designs of unbroken continuity: there is no end.

❦

During this period the sapsuckers visit one certain place more often than others. On the small hill sloping down to the lake three young white birches stand in close companionship. One bears the marks around its trunk just under a ring of branchlets of previous sapsucker borings now healed; another has been cut with an axe and a piece of bark stripped off the trunk; a third one has as a sapling sustained an injury which now forms a bulge from the healing effects of wood and bark grown over the scar.

76

During the spring and early summer the sapsuckers started vertical rows of holes in one or two of these trees. Now the birds return to these trees often. Presently they extend the rows until the birches are completely encircled by neat holes at even intervals. The clear sweet sap oozes through the holes; it wets and discolours the white bark. I call this the sapwell area.

To eat cambium, the tissue from which wood and bark are made, and to suck sap are basic needs of the sapsuckers. But it is not their only source of food. During the main part of the nesting season the extent to which the sapsuckers ate bast and sucked sap varied. Much depended upon the available supply of other foods — chiefly ants, beetles and moths, and also berries in season. And the abundance of the insects and fruits depended largely on the weather.

In the early spring, when the sapsuckers initiated the first borings in the sapwell area, bast-eating and sap-sucking were rather random occupations. True, the birds attacked a variety of trees but none too seriously. I found the characteristic rows of little holes perforating the trunks and branches of pines, balsam firs, spruces, oaks, ashes, alders — any tree, in fact, on which the sapsuckers happened to alight. And, according to the wealth of nutriments found, or the sapsuckers' whim, the birds either increased or abandoned these early perforations.

Then spring changed into summer and inaugurated the season of great swarms of insects. One insect population explosion followed upon another. All provided palatable substitute foods for bast-eating and sap-sucking. They filled the crucial needs of the sapsucker nestlings until the numbers of these insect populations again subsided. By the time the young sapsuckers were ready to leave the nest, the wild fruits were ripening, and the sapsuckers' great quest for insect food abated. The hustle, the labour and the excitement of the sapsucker nesting season had come to an end.

By this time the sapsuckers had gradually added more borings

77

on the trunks of the three birches at the sapwell area until the row of holes on one of the trees measured about six or seven inches in width. The sap running freely from the holes attracted other creatures than the sapsuckers. And with nature's overwhelming generosity there was plenty of it for them all.

The downy woodpeckers discovered the sapwells and came for quick licks undetected. Ruby-throated hummingbirds hovered in front of an oozing hole, withdrew, and returned to it again and again, lapping up the sweet stuff with their fantastically extensile tongues. Red squirrels clung spreadeagled across the bands of borings for prolonged drinks. The bees and the wasps coveted opportunities to crawl right into the wells of sweetness. With the exception of the renowned belligerents, the squirrels and the hummingbirds, the visitors practised little hostility among themselves. Most seemed willing to wait their turn, making only occasional attempts at displacing anyone that sipped too long or approached too closely to its neighbouring tippler. Only the sapsuckers that opened and maintained the commensal treat demanded and received due respect.

In relaxed seclusion Mar and his female cling solemnly to the trunks of the trees in their sapwell area. Mar shifts to the left. He taps and fashions another small, slightly squarish hole. He turns his head sideways and lets the sap run over his tongue into the groove of his lower mandible, savouring it with obvious satisfaction. He taps again and makes another hole. At every visit I find him hunched over his source of sweet nourishment, moving little except to adjust himself to take best advantage of the flow of sap that is descending from the top of the tree to the roots. In the adjoining tree the female clings to her band of borings in selfish oblivion of everything but herself and the running sap.

Every so often the young sapsuckers appear for a while at the sapwell. According to the mood, the adults chase them or ignore them. This does not bother the young ones, because by this time they have learned to find their own food. One may often see them launching themselves from high perches nimbly to snatch winged insects out of the air, flycatcher fashion. They extend these exercises also to the cherries and other ripe fruits they find hanging on the trees and shrubs. Hovering in front of the suspended tidbit, they dexterously snap it from the twig. But the attraction of the sapwell area is stronger than all else. And it is here, within the one or two acres that surround it, where every day I am able to account for each member of the sapsucker family.

Even before their young were fledged Mar and his female began showing signs of going into their annual post-nesting moult. Now loosened feathers are falling from their wings and tails one at a time, leaving awkward empty slots. Mar's brilliant red patches, his immaculate white lines and black markings become messy looking, his plumage loses its sheen. Obviously, the disarray of his feather makes him feel uncomfortable, for he sits burred up as if he were cold.

But all this passes, and by the middle of August an improvement is to be noticed in the appearance of the two old birds. The lost feathers are being replaced and the markings of their plumage gradually regain their former clarity of outline. The female's sudden appearance in full plumage by the middle of September takes me by surprise. It seems to have happened overnight. She looks smooth and shiny. Every detail of her satiny black and white markings is clear and distinct. And this has a curious effect on her behaviour. She withdraws from the sapwell area. She is not interested any more, she is free, moving around.

The young male's pink throat patch, I notice, has taken on a redder tint and where the black breast band of his mature plumage will edge his scarlet throat patch next spring, a black spot has appeared. The pearly fringe of the young female's white throat patch has vanished and soft white lines are beginning to show through the juvenile ashy colouring of her cheeks. These are significant plumage changes indicating a partial moult.

One or two mornings later I search in vain for the female and two of her daughters. During the past week migrating sapsuckers have been flitting through the forest on their way south and the lure of this movement was probably irresistible to those whose inner clocks were all set for departure. A day later the places of the precocious young female and her brother are empty.

Then the throngs of the migrating sapsuckers thin out and they are all gone amid the great flocks of other migrating birds. But Mar is still there, clinging to his oozing sapwells. Through a broad band of perforations he has dug a deep vertical groove. He sits there and with great concentration laps up the sap that seeps down the groove as in a miniature ditch. Does he ever move from this spot? It seems as if he cannot get enough of the sweet stuff. Does he ever feed or preen or do anything else but imbibe the whole day long? The fat under his skin accumulates.

The bracken has died. The shriveled brown leaves still cling to the stalks and rustle as I walk through them. The fallen leaves of the maples create a scarlet carpet under the naked branches. Only the golden leaves still deck the aspens and the birches in their full autumnal glory. The soft mosses underfoot are wet and shine emerald green. The first white frost comes one night, but as the sun rises the crystals quickly dissolve.

Mar is still at his sap groove. In full plumage now he has the polished brilliantined look of the early springtime when he put the mark of his presence imperiously upon the land.

The days grow colder and it rains often. On clear cool mornings white ground fog shrouds the forest and touches everything with clammy hands, leaving each strand of the spiders' webs delicately outlined with rows of tiny droplets.

In the evening of October 5 Mar is still at his sapwell. But the next morning the place is empty and dead. Sticky, cloying sap still runs down Mar's groove and drips on the white birch trunk, where it congeals.

# Chapter Eight

## The Young Against the Old

It is spring again—April 17. The air is crisp and clear in the early morning, refreshed and purified by the undisturbed exudations of the silent plant life during the night. The sun is shining, but is not yet far enough above the horizon to make its heat felt. Gray-green ice covers the lake. And where the ice has broken away, shallow open water full of dead leaves and rotting twigs separates it from the shores. A broad strip of ice-free black water runs down the middle of the lake.

A new sound suddenly pierces the air. I have been expecting it, half wistfully I have been waiting for it for several days already. I am not sure what the tidings will bring. It comes from the south end of the range Mar occupied last summer and four summers before that. The location call of the sapsucker—*here I am*—like the pumping of a pair of wheezy bellows, emphatic, insistent: *oh-weee, oh-weee, oh-weee, oh-weee*!

Who is that calling? Is it possible that it is Mar returning for the sixth time to this vast forested land where already during five summers he has lived and bred and raised his offspring? With every passing year the chances of a small woodland bird returning safely to his former territory decrease sharply. Tentatively I tap out my imitation signal: *ta-ta-ta*!

Listen! A sapsucker's rhythmic drumming in answer sounds loud and clear across the empty acoustic woods. Now I hear calling as well as drumming signals. Then a burst of clapping wingbeats! A sapsucker sweeps into the trees close by; it alights in the green aspen where last spring Mar started his first hole.

A red throat patch, and for a fleeting instant I catch sight of a shining aluminum band on the bird's left leg. Is it possible? I circle around the tree cautiously, lest the bird take fright and disappear. Through the silky fringe of soft belly feathers I glimpse a red band, encircling its right leg. The foot is lifted, he reaches under his wing to scratch behind his ear, and the red band, fully visible, falls back over the right tarsus. There can be no mistake. It is Mar.

The sedentary woodpecker—the hairy, some of the downy woodpeckers and the northern three-toed woodpecker—often reaches the ripe age of ten to fifteen years, spending the off-season period leisurely in comparative safety, with most of the predator hawks gone south and plenty of food secreted under the bark, in rotting trunks and stubs. Not so the migrating sapsucker. On the long journey to its wintering grounds which extend from Missouri and New Jersey to the Central Americas and the Caribbean islands, it runs the gamut of untold lurking dangers—sudden storms, pursuing predators and, not the least the confusing, illuminated man-made obstructions high in the air that kill thousands of night-flying migrating birds each spring and fall. For the migrating sapsucker six years is a long lifespan.

Mar drums a loud challenging signal. And, hearing and seeing him, I alone am able to appreciate the good luck that supported his wings during the long months of his absence from these woods, the extraordinary good fortune that led him through the hazards of migration back to his native grounds. He is back, having traveled directly guided by unerring instinct, possibly profiting by the previous twelve trips across the land to find his way back, alive until this day.

Like an arrow he darts away, head low, shoulders hunched. With an elegant swoop he alights on the crossbar of his favourite telephone pole. He crouches over the precise spot upon which are indented the weathered chisel marks of his earlier drummings. There he drums again, and the percussions cause the gleaming wires to tremble almost imperceptibly.

As if waiting for the next spring scene to open, cool silence and tranquility brood over the forest. Then one day the wind turns south and, suddenly, a new crowd of early migrants fills the region with movement, with twitter and song.

Among them are a few sapsuckers. The sight and sound of them galvanize Mar's hitherto dormant energies. Red crest erect, red throat ruffed, he criss-crosses the range, drumming and calling. His brown eye gleams as he puts his seal of priority upon these forested acres.

A day or two later, a strange sapsucker meanders into Mar's range. He moves about casually and unobtrusively. To my surprise he carries a blue band on his right leg above the numbered aluminum band, which identifies him him as a year-old bird hatched in the early part of last June in a neighbouring territory.

A young sapsucker returning to the native region to breed for the first time is not yet bound by territorial fidelity to any particular acres. Whatever memory of this area might have been imprinted upon the young sapsucker at the time when, during the two months after he left the nest, he roamed, fed and played there, probably little remained but a nebulous image. Yet his homing sense was strong and accurate, strong enough to drain from him the impulse to move on, to impel him to stop and to stay, there to carve out for himself a living room for the first time.

An encounter between Mar and the young one was inevitable and could not be long delayed. It began quite tamely with a drumming duel. Then with every passing moment fresh stimuli kept crowding in upon the two sapsuckers: the season was advancing, the spring migration of the birds was reaching its peak.

Transient sapsuckers, mingling with the other migrants, streamed across Mar's range to go on to disperse northwards or to settle on neighbouring territories. All this affected Mar's territorial drive, causing it to increase in vigour and vehemence. At the first sight of the young one Mar dashed at him, red crest stiffly erect, shivering slightly. They met on the nearest convenient tree trunk. And the inevitable demonstrations of threat and intimidation began with the usual posturings, the bill-pointing and the rhythmic jerky motions.

The two sapsuckers separate again, but the young one ignores all Mar's invitations to leave. The young one is not allowing himself to be so easily shooed away. Again the two opponents resort to an exciting, challenging tour of drumming. Atop one of Mar's favourite drumming posts the young one plays his resounding tattoo. Mar darts at him, violently unseats the intruder, then drums an emphatic signal on the very spot where the young one sat. It is impossible to mistake the meaning: This place is mine, get out!

The young one is stubborn—he is young and the engagement with the old one fires him with excitement. He dashes to another post and drums there. In a sweeping flight Mar catches up with his rival and drums. And so it goes from post to post, the young one defying the pretentions of the old one, the old one asserting them. Their staccato fanfares reverberate through the forest all day, as the tug-of-war over the land between these two sapsuckers rages unabated. At the end of the day the big question still remains unresolved. Which one shall possess the right of occupation on this land where Mar has lived and bred five consecutive seasons, and which for the sixth time he is now claiming for his own?

The next morning nervous tension visibly increases. Mar, the old one, the one with the tradition of residence to back him, is pitted against the young one who has nothing but the fresh strength of youth to back him. Every ounce of resistance that the old one puts up sharpens the drive in the young one, and he persists in challenging Mar's territorial rights. But Mar is not yet ready to yield one acre of land. The young one's obstinate assault upon his living room goads him to ever greater effort. And he drums his protest and relentlessly chases and pursues the rash young intruder in defence of his rights of prior possession.

Thus the battle between the old sapsucker and the young one goes on for three long days. It is strictly a private battle. In the midst of dozens of other birds, of untold numbers of creatures, all of which claim possession of at least part of the very same piece of land, it concerns no one but these two sapsuckers.

This is not a matter of species against species, but of individuals within the same species insisting on an adequate amount of space for food finding and breeding. The belligerency of the individual is not liable to involve members of other species except under particular circumstances, when population densities become too great, or when other pressures develop for some reason within one or several species, bringing about a variety of abnormal stimuli. The push of rising numbers, the frightening compulsions created by numbers multiplying beyond control, destroy the balance which neither judgment nor discretion, neither mercy nor sanity, can restore. The situation runs wild, it is chaos. The balance of nature is set very finely; it is exceedingly sensitive. It is in possession of innumerable resources by which intolerable upsets and pressures are counteracted in order to restore an equilibrium.

Mar's pursuits of the young one are spectacular in endurance and speed. With the intruder in the lead, and the old one never more than three wingbeats behind, the two antagonists shoot through the trees. On the fourth day the two of them slap their bodies smartly down on the horizontal branch of the great pine. There they stage a demonstration of aggressive-intimidating display of highest intensity. Both birds are trembling with nervous tension. The climax of their great struggle for supremacy seems at hand.

This time their displays do not dissolve as usual into a harmless session of feeding, preening and resting in order to catch their breaths and to revitalize flagging energies before a new round of sparring manoeuvres is due to begin again. This time they fly at each other with ferocious abandon. They clash in dangerous, reckless bodily contact hitherto circumvented so effectively by the displays, breast to breast, bills jabbing, claws flaying. And on the drafts of the fierce battle downy feathers, violently ripped from their follicles, sink softly to the ground.

Once again the birds fly apart and a chase ensues more protracted and spectacular than anything yet seen. One slightly ahead of the other, they dart through the tops of the trees, down through the undergrowth. I catch fleeting glimpses of them as, suddenly, a leaf here, another one there, is wafted violently by the turbulence of the air their race past sets astir. Their grasping feet simultaneously clasp a horizontal branch and another confrontation of aggressive displays takes place.

Suddenly they are no longer alone. Where the female came from nobody knows. Diffidently she clings to the branch not far from the combatants. She flattens herself against it, all her feathers smoothed tightly along her sides. As the two males in their urgent ritualistic demonstrations surge above her to and fro, she sidesteps lightly this way and that, never for a moment allowing the outline of her body to appear beyond the edge of the branch behind which she is hiding. If at this point some part of her actually did betray her presence, I have no way of knowing. Once again the two males join in fierce battle. They fall, fighting madly, but before they touch the ground, they fly apart and the chase is on again.

This time the race through the trees is of short duration. Back on the branch the two males go through a marvelous pantomime of posturings, advancing and retreating, the whole ritual of threat and contention. The female, no longer able to hide meekly behind the branch, emerges boldly and joins in the displays. She jerks her head right and left, flicks her wings, with an abandon as complete as the males', but not for long. She flies off, alights on an old aspen stub near by.

Suddenly Mar is aware of the female. The two meet on the stub. They perform their own partly aggressive demonstrations, slipping almost imperceptibly, perfunctorily, into an incipient version of the courting display, bobbing, facing each other. But again not for long. Abruptly the female breaks off the symbolic show and darts away.

The attraction of the female is too strong for Mar. He races after her, his head low between hunched shoulders, his wings beating fast in small, mincing, fluttering movements. And with this ritualized flight, he wins a mate and loses two acres of land.

❧

How logically nature always manages to provide for the smooth flow of continuity! As the coloured bits in the kaleidoscope fall together again in new patterns of perfect symmetry, so now the various events, pertaining to the rivalry between Mar and the young intruder, fall together quite naturally into a new pattern of apt coherence.

Had she been alive, Mar's mate of last year, the female who in the past two years had laid her eggs in his nest cavity, would surely have been back by now. Her homing instinct, her fidelity to established territory, had proved to be as true and as reliable as Mar's. She did not come, but many other females passed through, and one young one came, unattached to any previously established territory. It was a mere coincidence that she made her dramatic appearance in the midst of the males' fiercest territorial battle.

Nevertheless, it contributed in no trifling way to the turn of affairs. Since his own arrival in the early days of spring, Mar had plenty of opportunity to reach the required state of physical and psychological readiness for pairing. The excitements of his territorial difficulties only enhanced this reproductive readiness. And so, when the female beckoned, when she flew off enticing him to follow her into another tree, the struggle and the battle, the presence of the intruder, all counted for nothing.

Mar's new female immediately established herself on a piece of temporary territory across the road in the south part of his range. Her presence there allured him, and soon it awakened within him other half-forgotten, confused impulses. Hole-investigations, site-searching and nest-excavation began gradually to take precedence over his worries about the land. Not that these preoccupations made him abandon all territorial pretensions on the north acres, far from it. He still could not resist the temptation to make forages across the road to meet with the young one and stage inevitable inciting displays. But hole-boring and nest preparations require time as well as energy. And despite the female's constant intrusions upon his attention, exciting him with her frivolities and displays, he undertook these nesting activities. To some extent, therefore, these new interests caused a decline in Mar's defense of his territorial claims on the other side of the road.

This gave the young one his big chance. Although the land fell to him largely by default, he missed no opportunity to entrench himself firmly in the northern part of Mar's land. His persistence to remain which, in the face of Mar's violent opposition, he had so stubbornly displayed, now brought him his reward. He patrolled the land from one end to the other, red crest erect and red throat ruffed, tolerating the intrusion of no one of his own kind, be it transients or neighbours. He usurped Mar's drumming posts and established new ones for himself.

Wedged between the curving shoreline and the northern limit of Mar's original possessions north of the road, there was a small piece of land, a humid cedar dell grown with tall aspens among the evergreens. This land had for years belonged to the sapsucker pair resident on the extensive range to the northwest. Contention about this land brought the young one promptly into sharp conflict with the rightful owner.

If this land had not been only a spur extending quite far from the centre of the sapsucker pair's activities, had not the law been in force among birds that territorial belligerency diminishes the farther the distance from the centre, I doubt that the young one would have been able to assert his claims over it so cheaply. Yet, he had, it might be said, a certain right to it because the land acquired from Mar did not include all the requirements for a sapsucker's territorial range. The young one finally found himself the recognized sapsucker resident of an elongated forested area wedged between a cluster of well-established sapsucker territories on two sides and the lakeshore on the other two. This land contained two of Mar's previous nest trees, but not his sapwell area.

While spring migration lasted, many females passed through the domain of the young one. Although he made himself highly conspicuous the instant he spotted one of them, dashing from one tree to another, drumming and calling, none of these females showed any interest in him. Other goals lay ahead of them, long since established, to which some of them may have been returning for the second, third or even the fourth time. So they paid him no attention at all.

One morning a few days later I noted a surprising change in his behaviour. The conspicuous dashes across the range, the strut and the swagger had been abandoned. Curiously protracted silent periods alternated with shortlived bursts of calling and drumming. When I went to find out what he was up to, I found the young one engaged in a lively display with a white-throated female.

After a few preliminary aggressive displays, the young one broke off and in the usual seductive, fluttering flight moved a short distance away. The female alighted beside him, head high, crest erect and eyes gleaming. An exchange of soft mewing notes seemed to clinch the matter between them.

The next day I found the young one excavating a hole thirty feet up in the tree where Mar had nested the year before. The female had already evinced some interest in this tree; the old female's favourite drumming post had also pleased her and there she drummed, thus designating her choice of temporary territory.

The tree was too rotten; the ants had pulverized the disintegrating core and the brown dust poured from a small hole at the base of the trunk. So the young male turned his attention to the slender aspen by the lakeshore where Mar had started his first hole last spring. Twenty-four days later he had almost completed a roomy cavity ten feet above Mar's unfinished hole.

The young one had great difficulty persuading the female that the slender aspen was to hold their room for this season, but finally the female allowed herself to be brought around and lost no time putting her own chiseling bill to work deep inside. There, eventually, she laid her eggs.

On the fifth day, for some obscure reason, a strange restlessness took possession of the birds. Parent birds have an uncanny way of knowing when something is amiss. They react strongly; it upsets them. And a disturbance in their rhythm of activities causes immediately increased nervous tension.

Shifts were abandoned. The sitting bird lost its patience needed to await the arrival of the mate quietly and left the nest prematurely. In the half light on the bottom of the cavity the white eggs lay uncovered and unprotected.

It was a very tight doorway. How could a predator have penetrated past a recklessly defensive parent constantly on guard inside to steal one of the eggs? By what mischance did a would-be robber happen upon the nest at the precise moment when it was left unguarded? What subtle indication did the parents have of the loss of one single egg to cause their pronounced disturbance?

The next morning the female was missing. She had as usual visited the feeding station for her evening snack the night before. That was the last time she was seen.

How and when did this new calamity happen? Not in the nest, for the female slept elsewhere. And the loss of one egg the day before had no connection with the female's overnight disappearance.

The young male did not show any signs at first of missing the female. His behaviour followed the set incubation schedule for one partner. As usual he approached the nest sounding his mewing notes of mutual recognition, but there was no response. He entered, sat down and warmed the eggs as before in regular sessions of half an hour or more. When the female failed to relieve him, he left to rest and feed, and to deal with territorial affairs.

Gradually, however, the lack of the female's co-operation, her persistent absence, the coolness of the eggs when he returned from his prolonged recesses began to penetrate his awareness. The young one responded by increasing the tempo of his activities, by shortening his sessions on the eggs and by staying away for longer periods.

The eggs in the nest became colder and colder. Gradually the incubation pattern of the young male's behaviour dissolved and he reverted to his pre-nesting occupations, territorial advertising, calling and drumming.

❧

During the following three weeks the young male patrolled the range with great energy and enthusiasm. But no eligible female appeared, attracted by the sounds of his calling and drumming. Once Mar's female happened to stray across the border into the young male's territory. Greatly stirred by the sight of her, he immediately engaged her in animated display. Maybe it was something particular in the situation, maybe the timing, but somehow his display, his movements, lacked something of the usual persuasive force, for the female flew away and did not return.

Summer advanced and ripened. Newly fledged young birdlife filled the forest, everywhere. Slowly the reproductive drive of the young male waned. Slowly the preoccupations of his life, his behaviour, caught up with the normal trends and patterns of the season. His drumming subsided. He began to moult. Within the acre or so surrounding the two birch trees that he had long since designated as his main sapwell area, the young male became almost stationary. There he sat hardly moving and sucked the sap oozing from a broad band of holes until he had regained his full winter dress, until the time came for him, shiny and sleek, to fly south.

# Chapter Nine

## The Last Triumph

The miracle happened overnight. Warm air poured in from the south and spread over the spring-chilly landscape. The trembling aspens, the trees most sensitive to such cajolement, suddenly stood veiled in the sheerest verdure.

Mar was busy extending his decimated range farther to the south. In this environment he and his new female duly formed their first ritual attachment as a pair. This accomplished, the two of them turned their attention to other matters. The chilliness of the weather demanded a build-up of calories to reinforce depleted energies.

In the tops of the aspens dark, sticky rivulets of sap trickled along the stems of twigs and branches in natural overabundance. There Mar and his female, in separate seclusion hidden among the tender green lacework, gorged greedily upon the sweet running sap.

Once, the young male was seen slipping across the road from his newly established living room into Mar's area. No sooner did Mar catch sight of him than he was literally swept from the premises. This time no weakness, no hesitation, no matters conflicting with the urgency of defending his territory inhibited the action of the old male. A deeper territorial entrenchment

93

achieved by the passing of time and the afterglow of the famous fight, and the fact that the encounter with the trespasser occurred very close to Mar's centre of activities, combined to fire Mar's belligerency. Proximity stimulates motivation, and aggressiveness grows with motivation. The young male was never known to have repeated his mistake, nor was he seen even to skirt the outermost limits of Mar's private acres.

Suddenly Mar's preoccupation with old holes and cavities developed into an overriding urge. Such is the effect of the arrival of the female upon the activities of the sapsucker male in the beginning of the nesting cycle.

Looking for a suitable nest site, Mar soon yielded to the attraction of a tall, nearly dead aspen, around which the female had chosen to establish her "temporary" territory. A pair of hairy woodpeckers had inhabited a large, dark hole on the southwest side of the trunk a few years ago. Mar inspected the hole thoroughly. And in the benign environment of the female's choice, in a tree once before the home of a woodpecker, he began excavating a hole thirty feet from the ground and faced the doorway to the southeast.

Then, true to habit, Mar experienced a change of heart about the site. It seemed that, as was the case last year, the wood in this tree was not in the state of half decay required for a successful nest excavation. Sapsuckers' chisel-like bills are not so strong and efficient a hole-boring tool as the hairy woodpeckers'.

Mar started two new holes in different places, but abandoned both of these and finally settled for a large aspen past its prime high on a southeastern slope, not far from his sapwell area. He placed the doorway about forty feet up facing south, the direction from which the sun dispensed its most lavish gifts of light and warmth.

As might have been expected Mar's young female indulged in a variety of activities that effectively distracted him from his labours at the nest. She was only a year old, and consequently had

94

never been mated before. But she needed no instructions.

Her principal expression of concupiscence consisted of hovering around the nest tree, dashing away, calling and drumming, and then returning again. The sight of her invariably threw Mar into a state of high excitation. His head sharply inclined, beak pecking just under the breastbone, the bend of his wings dropped with the tips crossed over the rump, he *tap-tap-tap*-ed with rhythmic insistence on the lower edge of the doorway. Half submissively, half provocatively, the female alighted beside him with a resounding flop and sat, her body pressed to the trunk of the tree and the tips of her contour feathers lightly touching his. Mar's red throat trembled. His tapping increased in tempo and force. His body grew rigid and tense. For ten seconds he stood the rising tension. Then off he dashed squealing, his wings beating fast, shallow, the ritual fluttering flight. *Come on! Come on!* And the female, ever ready to respond, followed him in close pursuit.

Twenty-six days passed. Mar sat in the corridor of his all but completed cavity, his perky face framed in the doorway. He looked across the tree tops over the lake. By now all psychological barriers between him and his mate had been worn away. Time sufficiently allotted, punctiliously employed, promotes the successful development of nature's schemes.

❁

Behind the doorway, sheltered by a protruding knob, the incubation period of the sapsuckers progressed normally. Under the spreading crown of the aspen few enemies penetrated to discover the potential prey hidden deep down in the dim cavity. The rough gray trunk, seamed and weathered, possessed no formerly used holes to attract or harbour any unwelcome visitors. Occasionally a brightly coloured warbler or a demure red-eyed vireo might stray from ordinary nesting activities into the aspen's top to regale the listener with their songs.

95

The pleasing concert from above agreeably lulls the female sapsucker to sleep as she sits on the eggs. They exercise upon her an attraction greater than the nest itself. The touch of the warm smooth spheres against her developing broodpatch secures the bond between her and the progeny developing within the shells. This is the female's period of most consistent adherence to the nest, the only time during the nesting cycle when she is the more faithful attendant upon the nest and its contents.

The feel or the sight of the gnomelike creatures, tumbling helplessly from the broken shells as the eggs begin to hatch, causes the female to leave in quest of food before Mar arrives to relieve her. The smooth transition from the slow-rhythm mellow incubation period to the exploding presence of the living birdlings in the nest comes into effect at once. But the time the parents spend warming the hatchlings remains almost the same as the time they spent warming the eggs until the gradual development of the nestlings in the course of about three weeks makes such attention no longer necessary.

The quick response to change is natural balance—self-regulating, salutary, efficacious. It directs and shapes the lives of every living plant and creature, begets them, supports them, drives them, and eventually annihilates them. The interplay between creature and environment never functions at random, but always in narrowly logical sequences. It is the fundamental device that moves the microbe as well as the galaxy.

❦

Unpredictable! The calamity occurs when the young ones in Mar's nest are five days old. What befell Mar's young female I never knew. No tuft of torn feathers, no drop of red blood, left the faintest sign. In the morning she was there, bright, alert, busy. By noon she was gone.

The rhythm of the sapsuckers' activities about the nest at this stage of the nestlings' development may be translated in sequences something like this: out to forage—back with food—pop into gullet of nestling—brood ten to fifteen minutes—out—and repeat. The parents work together closely and the speed and timing of each is dependent in part on the speed and timing of the other.

Yet with the female gone, if Mar missed the cue of her presence and co-operation once or twice, it had for the moment no special effect on his behaviour. The impatient movement beneath him, the faint plaintive note of a famished nestling, provided enough stimulus to send him speeding out the doorway in search of food. Then an interesting adjustment occurred. With one of them missing, the parents' schedule of alternate attention upon the brood dissolves without causing any marked nervous upset. The change takes place smoothly with only a slight acceleration in the tempo of Mar's regular activities to meet the increased demand.

The safety and comfort of the young sapsuckers depend on two things: a sufficient provision of food and the inclination of the parent or parents to brood the nestlings adequately. The male sapsucker is able to fulfil these two conditions, because he is the one that sleeps with the young at night and the one that performs the greater share of the nest duties. This allows him without significant change of habits to function as two parents in one, thereby canceling out the loss of the female. In a reversed case the survival of the five-day-old nestlings would have depended mainly on the female's capacity for changing her sleeping habits, a major adjustment, to keep them warm at night.

During the next few days Mar manages the household affairs quite well. Although the pressure of attending to the needs of the nestlings increases slightly, he is able to take it in his stride.

Nevertheless, when the nestlings are eight days old, a certain change in Mar's behaviour is taking place. He is calling and drumming suspiciously often. These added activities prevent any acceleration in his feeding schedule. Perhaps some of the nestlings have ceased to respond to his ministrations because they are

97

either dying or dead? Conceivably such a situation might lessen Mar's motivation to forage and allow other impulses to come to the fore.

By the tenth day of nest life I am given plenty of evidence that Mar is busily feeding an unknown number of living nestlings at an accelerated rate of five and a half times an hour. Every so often he also hurriedly cleans out the nest. Sometimes he stays inside to brood the nestlings for periods varying from two to ten minutes. For the rest of the time he forages, sips some sap himself, and brings home portions just large enough to feed one nestling at a time. He performs this work fast and efficiently, and nothing disturbs him.

When the nestlings are seventeen days old, Mar's feeding rate has risen to thirteen meals per hour. This means that he brings food every four and half minutes, hardly allowing him much time to go far afield. The convenience of having the sapwell area so close, where furtive sipping supplies him with a good source of energy, is obvious. Apart from this, the mayflies are swarming, rising from the water in clouds to dance their gay figures among the trees and then alight on every twig and branch. The nestlings no longer require any brooding; it is doubtful if Mar broods them even at night, although he never fails to roost with them, clinging to the wall of the cavity.

Then, suddenly, a surprising and disconcerting situation arises. A strange female sapsucker appears upon the scene. The nestlings are now eighteen days old. She hitches up the trunk and passes around the doorway without looking in. And yet, she must have been aware of the life inside, moving and cheeping?

She is obviously unattached, for she moves about with the assurance of one newly arrived, seeking to set up "temporary" territory on a male's premises. She can do this boldly for no other female is there to oppose her. She is free to roam unchallenged and unmolested and takes good advantage of this freedom.

From his sapwell area nearby Mar has no difficulty seeing the female, but he makes no move to chase her away. She is there when he arrives at the nest. Without paying any attention to her, he goes in, feeds a youngster and comes out with a load of droppings dangling from his bill. In the usual manner he deposits it on the special tree trunk selected for the purpose. He darts back in and cleans out the nest three more times in quick succession. The nervous speed with which he performs these duties gives me the only inkling of his having noticed the female and is reacting to her.

Impetuous drumming and calling come from near the sapwell area, but I cannot see the originator of these noises. Mar darts to the nest — in, feeds, out. He repeats this routine six times. Four of the six times he snatches up a package of droppings while inside and flies out with it. The way he moves indicates a kind of frenzy that eloquently betrays the increasing nervous tension within him.

At this moment the female flops down beside the doorway, uninvited. She looks in but hops away again. Did she discover the nestlings within? She shows no sign, no impulse to pay them the slightest attention, let alone feed them. She clings to the trunk beside the doorway. As Mar arrives, she begins the full ritual tapping ceremony there at the edge of the doorway.

Now what? Usually enacted by both partners during the excavation as the nest is being prepared, the ritual implies developing impulses of sexual attraction and courtship leading to the consummation of sexual union.

As Mar arrives with his bill full of food, the female's behaviour bewilders him. Making no attempt to feed the nestlings, he darts away with the food still clamped in his bill. The female remains clinging to the doorway, scratching at her face, picking in her feathers.

The attraction of the nest, the pressure of the feeding impulse and the tension created by the female's presence, play havoc with Mar's routine. In a series of frenzied feedings, he dashes past the

99

female to and from the nest, in and out with minute, quickly snatched meals, while she still clings at the doorway. This causes a redirection of his frustrated energies. The distant chatter of a squirrel, a warbler innocently trespassing, he now objects to strenuously. He chases a sapsucker neighbour foraging at a distance, whose presence never before bothered him because he was too busy. Then he undertakes another series of nine frenzied feedings at incredible speed, cramming hardly visible meals from his all but closed bill into the gapes of the nestlings huddled far back in the corridor.

Naturally, the stress created by this frantic situation is bound to reach the saturation point. Often, as a crisis reaches a point just short of climax, a deflector of some kind appears that diverts the frustrated feelings and eases the tensions. An unexpected distraction momentarily relieved the strain, the female temporarily disappeared, and the hard-pressed parent bird was given needed breathing spells, allowing him to resume a still very fast but more regular pace.

Mar reaches his top performance in attendance on the nest during the following days by bringing the nestlings twenty to thirty meals an hour. This means that within two or three minutes he is able to capture enough insects to fill his bill, to drench the mouthful in sap at the sapwell area, to dash to the nest and pop the meal into a waiting gape and depart. He maintains this amazing pace over periods of hours without rest, a truly breathless performance. Measure the degree of adaptability and sensitive response required of a parent bird that suddenly becomes the sole provider for a nestful of growing offspring to keep them alive over a period of several weeks, and Mar's stamina and flexibility are readily assessed!

The strange female's lack of response to Mar's begging nestlings is surprising. Not even Mar's untiring shuttle service with his bill full of food inspires her with any impulse to do the same. Gaping and begging young birds usually act not only upon any parent bird, but also invite unmated and unproductive birds to feed them, and seldom fail to elicit a response. There are innumerable examples. A female Blackburnian warbler with her bill full of food hastily fills the gaping mouths of a nestful of myrtle warblers she happens to pass by on her way to her own nest; an unmated white-throated sparrow assiduously assists a pair of her own species to raise their brood; a sapsucker female so eager to feed someone that she insists a red-breasted nuthatch take the offering she is forcing upon it. But this strange sapsucker female—no, not she! Never once did she make any attempt even to enter Mar's nest, much less bringing any food to his nestlings within.

As the time approaches for Mar's youngsters to leave the natal cavity, a change occurs in the behaviour of the strange female. She still courts him, but there is a slight moderation in her fervour. The passing of time and season? The lack of sexual response? Are these the reasons?

The nestlings are at the doorway, clamouring for food and attention. Mar, driven by these pressures, pays scant attention to the strange female; he squeezes past her to the doorway, fills the panting gape inside and flies away. A squirrel runs up the trunk of the nest tree. Red crest on end, Mar shoots out of nowhere upon the hapless animal like a demon, screaming, striking with bill and claw. The next instant he disappears into the nest hole. Pushing the nestlings before him back into the cavity, he turns and takes up an ambush position just inside the doorway, his awl-like beak at the ready. The frenzy that marks his movements and his violent reactions to ordinary everyday threats, to any incursion upon the circumscribed space around his nest tree, reveals the nervous tension that builds up within him every time he sees the strange female. And only as he clings to the doorway close to his own progeny, all conflicting motivations fall away from him and he meets the proximity of his clamouring youngsters with the feathers on his head smoothed down flat, his eyes large and gleaming, bill meeting bill in the transference of his offering of food.

The twenty-seventh day of nest life slips by and Mar's youngsters are still in the nest. But in the afternoon of the twenty-ninth day, four weeks and one day after the eggs hatched, two nestlings fledge, leaving the nest empty.

Mar's natural experiment raising his family alone after the demise of his mate when the nestlings were only five days old is at last completed. For four weeks he toiled almost unceasingly in response to the doubled demands suddenly thrust upon him. And although his paternal capacities were insufficient to cover the needs of all the nestlings that hatched, carrying through to safe fledging only two of them, and although this took him three days longer than normally required, nevertheless his efforts must be considered highly successful.

❧

It is mid-July. Mar's fledglings have been served their last meal from the fatherly bill. What still holds the family together is the land, through the bond between the old bird and his territory, and the young birds and their native forest.

Mar is in full moult. Feathers loosen and fall from him, leaving bare spots, ruffed and uneven edges. He looks ragged and exhausted. He moves little. Most of the time he sits hunched over his sapwells that encircle the white trunk of the birch, partly hidden under a spray of green leaves. Day after day, hour by hour, he clings tightly to the trunk of the tree and sips the sweet colourless fluid oozing from the holes.

The leaves of the trees turn into gorgeous hues of blood-red, gold and russet. They reach their full blaze of autumnal glory. And when the colours begin to fade, Mar is still there. The last migrating sapsucker came meandering through the forest almost two weeks ago, southbound. A cold wind runs through the dry rustling leaves, and they fall softly whirling to the ground. But Mar still does not take the hint.

That night I saw Mar for the last time. He was in full feather, sleek, smooth, glistening, as if his plumage had been lightly brushed with oil. Every marking on his back, on his shoulders and flanks were pencil-sharp, perfect in line and design. Every colour, the white, the black, the scarlet and the subtle sulphur-coloured wash over his sides and belly, was clean and distinct.

I would not speculate on when, how it happened. So far but no farther, that is the clear justified limitation of all things alive, the only way for each to contribute its essential, unique existence, due inexorably to disappear and be replaced.

## WOMAN BY THE SHORE

There is a woman
I know, at Pimisi Bay
who says she's getting old
whose brave words
make me cry
when I thought I was through
with crying:
"I have reached
the all but obscene
age of 90 ... said in the sense,
that to reach for the exaggerated,
is to challenge the rational."

Little wonder that there are
tears on my face;
Louise speaks with clarion voice
and utter sensibility
for all of us.

I see her now
on a bench beside the bay
bird calls drawing her
out of herself,
words streaming through
her serene mind
a desire to write
making her blue eyes shine.

Listen to the loon
dear lady, let the voice of
the white-throat
send you my love.

Robert W. Nero
April 2, 1984

www.ingramcontent.com/pod-product-compliance
Lightning Source LLC
Chambersburg PA
CBHW050536280326
41933CB00011B/1610